# Shiatsu for your horse

To my children
Adam, Daniel, Gemma and Jake
Thanking them for putting their lives on hold
whilst I created this book.

Cathy Tindall

## Acknowledgements

The authors would like to thank Selina Boyce for the use of her smallholding as a location for our photography and for the use of her exceptional horse, Bill; Barrett for the use of his youngsters; and Rachel Upton for being so helpful and delivering and collecting Dolly and Chips, neither of whom were an embarrassment to her!

We would also like to thank Paula Gautrey for the use of her yard and Lisa Kinch and Jo Abbott for coming out on a cold and miserable day with Millie and Mac respectively.

## Disclaimer

The authors and publishers of this book would like to make it known that in no way are any of the techniques described intended as an alternative to veterinary consultation and treatment. If you are ever in doubt about the health and well-being of your horse, please consult an equine veterinary surgeon.

The authors and publishers of this book recommend that all due safety measures associated with the care and attention of horses, including hard hats and protective footwear, be used as appropriate whenever in the presence of an equine. The authors and publishers shall accept neither liability nor responsibility for any damage, accident or injury purported to result from following the procedures detailed in this book. Whilst every effort has been made to ensure that the information contained herein is accurate, there may be omissions, errors and inaccuracies.

Copyright 2006 by Cadmos Verlag, Brunsbek
Typesetting and design: Ravenstein, Verden
Front cover: Angus Murray
Photos: Angus Murray
Print: Westermann Druck, Zwickau
Edited by Jaki Bell

Published in Germany

ISBN 3-86127-915-0

# Shiatsu
## for your horse

Enhance your horse's well-being and happiness

Written by Cathy Tindall and Jaki Bell

# General Introduction

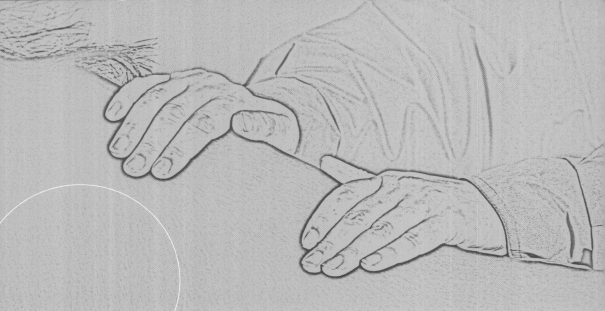

"In writing this book I hope to be able to bring to every horse person the ability to give a reasonably knowledgeable Shiatsu treatment. This book has several uses, depending on your desire. Firstly, it may be taken as a guide to empower you to make your horse feel well and full of joie de vivre. You can then move on and take in a little more, gaining a basic knowledge of muscles, bones and other anatomical and physiological aspects. Finally you can learn the various ways that a Shiatsu practitioner would assess where to start a treatment and what to treat. I have also intended the knowledge contained in this book to address the course requirements of my year one students and thank them all for their input into structure and style.

## How did I get here today?

Fifteen years ago I came across Shiatsu in a tiny advert in the local paper suggesting its benefit for sports injury. I had a nasty riding accident that left me in a chair for six weeks. I was finding breathing extremely difficult and had tried all other 'normal' therapies. I decided that I needed some more effective help. This is when Shiatsu came into my life. Whilst I was having treatments myself, lying on the floor on a futon, pondering this amazing therapy, it dawned on me that if this therapy worked so well on humans, who have the ability to block its effectiveness with their brain, how would it work on horse's who live for the moment and know what they need in order to heal?

Having had this thought, to begin this life-altering training I needed to find someone able to instruct me and to help me pass this knowledge on to others. That quest took 10 years now The College of Natural Equine Studies runs a tESA recognised two-year practitioner course, which anyone may attend as long as they have a love of horses and a desire to learn and to give something back. I will soon have my first practitioner in the Netherlands (Tista).

## What inspired me about Shiatsu?

Shiatsu was the one therapy that I had received that did not include the cracking of bones, getting undressed and the fact that I would need to be treated for many years. Although in my particular case the Shiatsu treatment was targeted at my back, it left me feeling amazingly good. I began to sleep at night and a little weight began to drift off. My skin looked healthier and my digestive system seemed to be working better than it had in years. All in all this therapy seemed to me to be a miracle and something I wanted to pass on to horses. After all, along with equine domestication comes ailments and stress, that horses feel just as much as we humans.

As I treated more and more horses I began to realise that this was a wonderful way of working with such forgiving creatures. I also saw improvements in the horses' well-being. Some horses became less spooky, others less colicky. Some of the horses who had been intermittently lame became progressively more sound, whilst others just appeared much happier. And the list goes on. Shiatsu can have an amazing ability to get under the skin. For example, one of my students (Kate) surprised an owner by asking what bereavement her horse had recently suffered. The owner hadn't told anybody about the companion her horse had lost!

Today Shiatsu is a big part of my life. Apart from running my course in the UK, I travel throughout Europe to wherever I am invited to lecture and treat. I also use Shiatsu in my day-to-day work as an Equine Behaviour and Health Consultant. It is useful to find out where issues lie and it gives me an idea of what I need to use in order to help the individual horse.

I would like to think that through this book and my courses I will bring Shiatsu into the reach of every horse person, all over the globe. Not only will this benefit the health of each individual horse but it will help the horse/handler relationship. The giver also benefits when giving a Shiatsu treatment! I also hope that by teaching people to really listen to the likes and dislikes of the horse it will make them a better and a more considerate horseman or woman and, over all, that the benefits of Shiatsu to the horse will become obvious to all."

Cathy Tindall

# Contents

# Part 3: An introduction to the meridians via The Five Elements . . . . 46

# Part 4 Appendices . . . . . . . . . . . . . . . . . . . . . . . . . . .124

# Part 1

# Giving a Shiatsu massage

## What is Shiatsu

*Shiatsu is a healing touch therapy that originated in Japan.*

Around the middle of the fifth century BC Buddhism was introduced to Japan from China and with it came an influx of Chinese medicine, philosophy and culture. Chinese medicine was tightly interwoven with religion and philosophy and many Chinese medical practices were of a preventative nature. In ancient China, a doctor was only paid as long as his patient was healthy; as soon as the patient became ill the doctor's income dried up.

The Japanese took two Chinese therapies anma (massage) and acupuncture and developed Shiatsu, which in Japanese means finger pressure and is regarded in

Western cultures as Japanese physiotherapy. Shiatsu has evolved as a traditional Japanese bodywork therapy based on pressure and stretches and is as popular today as ever it was. It works the same points of the body that acupuncture stimulates using needles, and is sometimes incorrectly compared with or referred to as acupressure. However, unlike acupuncture, Shiatsu only uses the pressure from hands, fingers and elbows to create the stimulus that is needed.

One of the great things about Shiatsu is that, with the most basic of knowledge, anyone can use it. We all have the ability to heal with our hands. Sceptical? How often did you hear the words from your mother: "Let me rub it better"? Have you ever enjoyed a massage? Think of the comfort you gained as a child from the touch or stroke of your mother's hand. What is your immediate reaction when you see someone in distress? Even despite the restrictions imposed upon us by society today, most people will, at least, reach out to touch, at best put an arm around the person suffering. These are primitive instincts coming to the fore.

How does it work?

Shiatsu works on two levels:
Firstly it acts on a physiological level. By working on the body with pressure and stretches we can have a profound effect not only on the circulatory, lymphatic and nervous systems, improving blood flow and vitality, but also on the major organs of the body. The skin is the body's largest organ. Touching the skin and the underlying nerves at specific points around the body releases the body's own pain-dampening hormones, endorphins, and can have an incredibly calming effect, releasing stress and tension.

The second level is more spiritual. The principals of Shiatsu are based on the belief that energy (Chi) flows through the body on a specific network of channels known as the meridians. When a wound heals itself, this is Chi at work. Chi should be free-flowing, however stress and illness cause the channels, or meridians, to become blocked. The Chi ceases to flow and the balance of well-being is interrupted.

The meridians

These meridians (twelve on each side of the body) are the framework by which oriental medical theory provided the practitioner with a means to assess the body's energetic state and needs. The meridians connect together to form one circuit of energy, supplying all the cells in the body. They also offer an explanation why the body holds tension in some areas and feels weakness in others.

Each meridian is named after a particular organ. Its relationship to that organ goes beyond just the basic function. Let me draw the following parallel: the meridian is like a piece of music with the body organ as the crescendo, the climax. Whilst a meridian may be named after one body organ, its effect can be felt by many.

It is along these meridians that the Shiatsu practitioner works, using a combination of stretches and movements with the hand, fingers and elbows and focussing on the quality of the energy that flows through the meridian. The practitioner will work from the beginning of the chosen meridian to the end, freeing blockages or dams (Jitsu) and stimulating weaknesses or stagnant pools of energy (Kyo). The presence of Jitsu and Kyo may lead to physical symptoms or psychological and emotional disturbances. Jitsu, which manifests as heat, shows up as tight muscles and areas of stiffness. Kyo feels cold, weak or just inspires a need to hold.

For centuries now, Shiatsu has been used to promote health and spiritual well-being for mankind; now these benefits can be shared with your horse.

## How Shiatsu can help your horse

Whilst most of our equine partners have dealt with domestication, horses often suffer from stress caused by practices we employ in caring for them that are contrary to their biological needs. Shiatsu is a healing method with which you can give something back to your horse.

Twenty years ago had you mentioned that your horse was to see the physiotherapist you would have been laughed off the yard. Now most equestrians appreciate that horses can benefit from alternative therapies in much the same way as their owners. This is perhaps the right moment to say that Shiatsu is never an alternative to a visit from the vet and you should always inform your vet if you are considering using Shiatsu in conjunction with prescribed treatments. However once you are aware of a problem and treatment has been suggested, or as part of a general maintenance programme for your horse, working physiologically and psychologically, Shiatsu can help with the following:

- It can relax and de-stress the horse (allowing the body a better chance to heal itself)
- It can counter spookiness
- It can ease depression and aggression
- It can ease tired and overworked muscles
- It can help with sore backs, sprains and strains
- It can ease poll, neck and shoulder stiffness
- It can ease joint pains
- It can help with hormonal imbalances
- It can improve a low resistance to infection
  And the list goes on…

Shiatsu can also help develop a better relationship between horse and owner and can have a positive health benefit for both as it has a two-way effect - if it feels good to you, it will feel good to your horse.

In these busy times, giving a Shiatsu massage can also create some quiet, quality time for you and your horse to spend together, with nothing better to do than experience each other's presence.

## Listening skills

When you call out your vet, the first thing you will be asked is what you think is wrong with your horse. You will probably recount one or two things you have observed that were not normal for your animal. You would have come to these conclusions using your senses of sight, sound and touch plus your 'gut feeling' or intuition. It is these same senses that you use when you come to work with your horse with Shiatsu.

There are obvious physical indicators of the way a horse is feeling: most people know what is indicated by the position of the ears or the way the eyes look, but have you ever taken much notice of the muzzle and the edge of the nostrils?

The muzzle can show tension by being tight and having lots of wrinkles around it. If the horse is relaxed the skin will be loose and floppy.

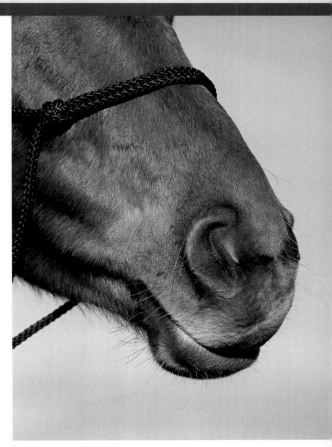

*Tight nostrils usually indicate tension in your horse.*

If the nostrils are very taut and defined around the edge, that can indicate tension or irritation but if they are soft and floppy, with no defined edge, this suggests that the horse is at ease and relaxed.

Watch your horse's breathing pattern. If this changes and he either begins to breathe more quickly or slower it will signify a change in attitude or demeanour – look for what is going on.

Look at the way your horse stands when tied up. Is he relaxed with a low head carriage and resting hind leg or is he uncomfortable, possibly in pain and agitated, which might be indicated by restlessness, a high head carriage and a stamping foot?

Remember every body movement expressed by the horse means something. He is doing it on purpose in order to communicate how he is feeling. He is not just being downright awkward.

## The jigsaw puzzle

Once you are aware of these methods of communication, you must be very careful how you process the message. It is important to look at all the signals and not one alone. By looking at, say, just the ears you could get the wrong impression of what is going on for the horse.

Let's say you are looking at a new horse and he has his ears back – what would that suggest to you?

It could mean that he is irritated, frightened, aggressive or just listening to what is going on behind him. In order to get the true meaning you must look for other signs.

For example, if he has his ears back but has large, soft, open eyes, his breathing is slow and he is resting a hind leg, would you be afraid of this horse? Probably not. However what about the horse in the next stable that also has his ears back, but has a raised respiration rate, tight nostrils and is lungeing at you over the door? Well, you work it out.

So think of the act of listening to your horse as one of creating a jigsaw puzzle - without all the pieces you will not have the complete picture.

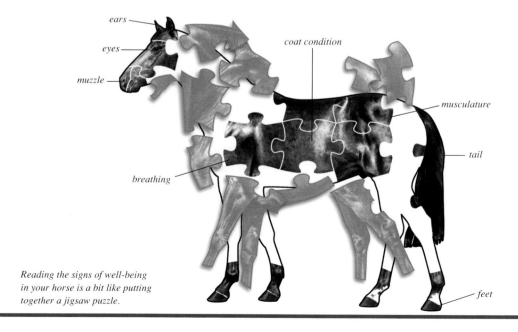

*Reading the signs of well-being in your horse is a bit like putting together a jigsaw puzzle.*

*Close your eyes and run your hands over your horse's body. See if you can feel what his body is trying to tell you.*

Signs that your horse is happy and relaxed:

- soft fluid eye
- droopy nostrils and lips
- body still with relaxed muscles
- resting a back hoof
- head low
- eyes semi-closed
- sighing
- yawning

Signs that your horse is anxious, uncomfortable or unhappy:

- swishing of tail
- abrupt stamping of feet
- ears back
- eyes becoming small, wide or just changing from the relaxed state
- nostrils tightening/wrinkling
- pursed or tight mouth
- quick licking and chewing
- excessive self grooming
- moving away from pressure
- yawning

## Using your intuition

How many times have you used your intuition or 'gut feelings' in judging circumstances or deciding upon a course of action? The most common example for all of us is in making a spontaneous decision about an individual upon first meeting them. Sometimes we get it right, sometimes not so. Those of you who are 'in touch' with your intuition will know it. It is something you learn to trust with experience. It can also be developed and, as you become more accomplished in Shiatsu, if you allow it to happen, your intuition will evolve. It is an important tool in assessing what is needed during a Shiatsu massage. As you run your hands over your horse's body, you will learn to allow them to go where they want, to spend a little more time in one area than another. A good exercise is to close your eyes and run your hands over your horse. Feel what his body is telling you.

## Two-way communication

As humans we are too good at imposing our will on animals without checking with them that it is okay and they like it. When you touch or groom your horse do you check that he likes what you are doing?

Shiastu is a quiet therapy and your horse will love most of what you do, but do listen to him because he knows his body best. If he moves away, he probably doesn't like what you are doing. However this dislike may not be of the treatment or necessarily the meridian that you are working on but could be:

- the pressure that you are using,
- the way your touch feels (it could be tickly)
- the spot you are on in that particular meridian

Horses also know what meridians they NEED working on and if you pick the wrong one for your horse, he will let you know. As you get to practice you may notice that your horse prefers to receive his Shiatsu at a particular time of the day. Just like humans some horses are morning animals and others prefer the afternoon or evening. Discover and utilise the time that your horse likes best for your Shiatsu treatment. This timing will be further explained in Part 3.

## Displacement behaviour

We have taken a look at the equine language in order to determine whether our treatment is being appreciated or not. Now we need to look at a form of language that may seem to be contradictory. This is called 'displacement behaviour'.

Displacement behaviour is totally natural for the horse to do but is performed in the wrong place, at the wrong time, with no apparent benefit. Such as:

- licking and chewing
- playing with the tongue
- yawning
- rope chewing
- pawing the ground
- lowering the penis
- constant rolling
- wood chewing for long periods
- bar scraping with the incisors

and anything else that you may see that seems like inappropriate behaviour at that time. This usually takes place in response to conflict situations and indicates agitation, or a dislike of what is happening at that moment in time.

As you can see from this list, you can quite easily misinterpret some of these signs, so make sure you use the jigsaw to help you determine what is going on. For instance if you are gently grooming your horse in the sunshine and he has his eyes semi-closed and his head lower than his withers, you can interpret that any slow licking and chewing is contentment. However, if you are trying to urge your wide-eyed, head-high horse through a stream and he begins to lick and chew you can assume that he is agitated and in conflict, not wanting to do what you are asking.

When a horse is agitated, being a prey animal his instinct is to run away. If circumstances prevent him from doing this, he has to perform some physical act in order to use up the flight hormones that have been rapidly released into his blood system. This is when you may see one of the aforementioned activities taking place. On a human scale this is like having a panic attack – if vigorous exercise is taken at the onset of a panic attack, the effects of the attack will diminish and you will feel much better.

Whilst giving a Shiatsu treatment you may find that when you move onto another meridian, or indeed another point on the same meridian, the horse will lick and chew. Check all the other visual signs to see if this is positive licking and chewing (meaning that he likes it) or negative licking and chewing (meaning that he does not). In my experience the negative licking and chewing is more rapid than the languid lick and chew

of a horse that is appreciating his treatment. You may find that you see this more when you come to the stretching part of your treatment, especially if the horse is unable to balance very well.

Remember that displacement behaviour and signals are another way the horse can tell you whether or not what you are doing is acceptable.

# Preparing yourself and your horse for a treatment

## Before you begin

As I have already said, anybody can give a Shiatsu massage. However the more 'in touch' you become with your own energies and those of the horse, the more effective your massage will be. It is possible just to learn the physical movements and use them to the benefit of your horse but I firmly believe that anyone using Shiatsu for any length of time will want to understand more about what is going on.

I would therefore recommend that before giving a massage you take time to prepare, or centre, yourself as well as your horse. This takes the treatment from a practical, physical treatment to one that has more depth, power and harmony. There are two ways in which this can be done.

*By connecting with your Hara you will be able to amplify the benefits of Shiatsu.*

### The Hara

The Japanese believe the Hara to be the whole soft area bounded by the ribs and the pelvic bone, both posterior and anterior. This is your centre and it is from here that you sense your 'gut feeling'. It is the development of the Hara that furnishes the giver with increased stamina and enhanced energy and a better ability to sense and affect Chi.

So how do you do this? Sit or stand in a comfortable position (if standing, have your feet hip distance apart and your knees slightly bent). Place your hands on top of your stomach. Now just listen to and feel your own breathing pattern. Don't change anything, just let it happen. Once you are in tune with your own natural breathing begin to allow the breath to go down into your stomach and, as you take each breath, feel your hands rise and fall. When you have achieved this, begin to visualise the airflow coming in through your nostrils and moving all the way down; imagine it as a golden light filling the stomach with pure golden energy. With each breath visualise more and more energy coming into the body and filling the stomach until you have harnessed your Hara and are able to work from it and with it.

### Chigong

Another way of working with your own energy is by practising Chigong. Translated this means "energy combined with skill" and the technique is practised in yoga, martial arts and even by the Shaolin monks, who seem to perform incredible feats of martial art skills, and live to a ripe old age.

What does Chigong do? It helps to balance the energies that course around the body allowing you to feel more centred and grounded. This in turn helps you to give a deeper and more personal treatment to your horse.

Chigong is very easy to achieve and anyone can do it. (Although if you are suffering from any ailment please consult your doctor before embarking on Chigong as it can be very powerful and is contra-indicative in pregnancy.) It is generally performed in the standing position but can be done sitting in a chair or even lying down.

Begin by standing, sitting or lying in an area that is quiet and comfortable. Make sure that your feet are warm and preferably shoeless. Have your hands by your side and your feet together.

Keeping your heels still, turn your toes out 45 degrees.

Now turn your heels out level with your toes.

Turn your toes out once again 45 degrees. And finally turn your heels out so that your feet are facing forward.

This is your resting position.

Bend your knees slightly and open your arms in front of you as if you were hugging a great big oak tree. Have your palms facing you, your thumbs relaxed and your shoulders lowered. Breathe evenly and make sure that you do not tense up.

Remain in this position initially for 5 minutes. Your target is to gradually increase the time you can remain so to about 45 – 60 minutes. Sometimes it is hard to get started and you may find that you begin to feel aches or pain, perhaps from some old injury, in stiff joints or in any other part of your body.

If you feel faint, close off by bringing your arms up and over your head with clenched fists, whilst breathing out. If you feel the need, also have a drink of water.

Working with Chigong you should begin to feel great health benefits and wonder why you have not heard of it before. The more you do the more you will be able to contact the inner you and begin to use your existing intuition. There are now many classes available in Chigong.

## When and where to give the massage

Your first step is to find a quiet period in the activity at your yard. Choose an area in which your horse feels calm and comfortable, and where you will both be safe. As a general rule, horses that are kept out should find being outside more comfortable and those that spend a lot of time in a stable might find this option more attractive. However this does not always hold true so watch and listen to your horse to find the best place for him.

You could try asking yourself where he prefers to be groomed. Alternatively, try tying him up in several places to see where he appears to be most settled. In the stable, without the distraction of hay nets or feed buckets, allow him to 'settle' and make a note of where he does so. If he chooses the same spot on two or three occasions, this will be his 'comfort' area and the space in which to treat him. If you are practising Shiatsu in a stable, check for dangerous objects such as protruding nails, buckets that you both may fall over, or rug straps that you may trip on and remove them.

If your horse is not groomed, don't worry, cleanliness may be next to Godliness as far as we are concerned but the horse really doesn't mind what state he is in for a treatment. Brush off the dirt that really clings on, but don't worry about anything else. (You'll find that your bare hands are a good grooming tool.)

On occasion you may find that a horse, whilst appearing to enjoy the Shiatsu, shows a strong reaction to the contact of your hands. If this is the case, you can actually treat through a rug. A thin summer sheet would be best but I have treated through a New Zealand. You could also try wearing gloves.

## After the treatment

When working with Shiatsu we begin to change and enhance the energy flow, not only through the horse but through ourselves as well. Although there should not be an exchange of energy, someone giving a Shiatsu massage is often left with an empathetic feeling, either good or bad, which may have originated from the horse. To cleanse yourself of this feeling you need to do what is described as 'grounding'. In the

early stages of massage you can do this by either putting your hands onto an outside wall and holding them there for a few seconds, by washing your hands in cold water or by clapping your hands three times.

Once you begin to experience this empathetic feeling to a greater degree or regularly, it is time for you to start to protect yourself before you begin a treatment. Below are a couple of examples of ways in which you can do this, but there are many others. With a little imagination, I am sure you will find methods that will suit your personality and skills.

As you are preparing yourself to give a treatment imagine:

• that you are enveloping yourself in a large golden balloon, the light from which is so intense and pure that nothing can penetrate it. Like a balloon, it can mould to the touch and thus allows your hands to continue the treatment without coming into direct contact with the horse

• that you are a rose bud. You still have the beauty and fragrance of the open rose but you also have strength and, because your petals are closed together, you will not allow any negative feelings to get in.

Yellow is a good colour to work with in this context. A friend of mine told me of a fellow healer who had painted the front door frame to her house yellow. She imagined that as she walked through it, her protective veil enveloped her. These may all sound a bit wacky but they are methods that have been used by thousands of healers worldwide throughout the years and have stood the test of time.

## When you should not give a Shaitsu treatment

If your horse:
- has a high fever – seek veterinary advice
- has just had a strenuous workout – wait until he/she has cooled down properly
- has had recent surgery
- has an infectious disease – seek veterinary advice
- is pregnant
- is a stallion and has just covered a mare - wait at least 12 hours before giving Shiatsu.

If you:
- are too tired
- are intoxicated
- have a skin or air contact contagious disease
- do not want to give a treatment – (Ask yourself why?)
- are unsure about the efficacy of Shiatsu for this horse.

## What does energy feel like?

This is the million dollar question as it feels different to each individual. Beneath your hands you may experience many different feelings as you work with Shiatsu and your abilities grow. I feel as though I am floating in the air and looking down at the situation.

The energy could feel like:
- A tingling sensation
- A pulse
- Fizzing
- A movement that goes from one hand to the other
- A feeling of nausea
- A floating feeling
- A faint feeling

Try this exercise:
Stand up and vigorously rub your hands together for a full minute. Then, with legs bent, hold your hands out as if you were holding a small ball. Regulate your breathing and then gently bounce your hands apart and together with small, gentle movements. Do you feel anything? If you feel that there is a 'ball' between your hands or that there is something there that feels like a repulsion of magnetic fields, you've got it.

Some of you will have a reaction and some of you won't. What's important is that it doesn't matter, you can still give a treatment. The feeling will come with time and experience.

And remember, whatever you feel or don't feel is what is right for you and your horse at the time. Be patient, Rome was not built in a day and all good things come to him, or her, that practises!! It took me years to allow myself to feel energy but I still treated many horses with fantastic results.

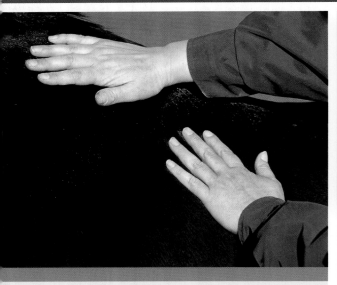

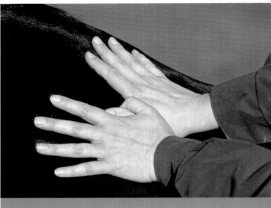

### 3. Butterfly
Link your thumbs together and splay your fingers. Then, making circular movements, work all over the horse's body. You will find that on certain parts of the body you are working against the natural direction of growth of the hair – some horses will not like this.

### 1. Body sweep
Using both hands, hold as shown, and 'sweep' them lightly over the horse's entire body.

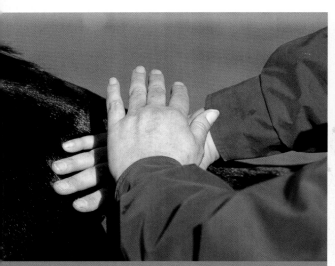

### 2. Hand-over-hand energiser
Holding your hands as above, place one hand over the other in a rapid movement to wake up energy and circulation.

### 4. Joint sweep
Using the same movement as the Body sweep, work across, round and up and down all joints.

### 5. Body rock

Cup your hands over the spine and using your body weight, rock backwards and forwards. You will find that this rock will extend down the length of the body. If you find it difficult it might mean that there is a blockage of energy flow somewhere. Finish with a tail glide.

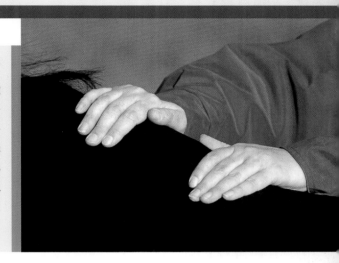

### 6. Tail glide

Stand to the side of our horse. Take his tail out of the crease it sits in and gently pull down along thin lengths of tail hair (see page 31).

### 7. Neck rock

This is similar to the body rock, but you use your fingers on the other side of the neck to gently but firmly pull the crest towards you.

## 8. Percussion

There are three percussion movements:

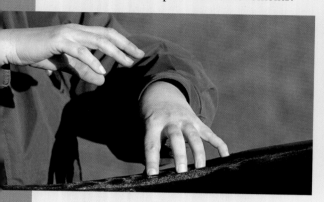

a. Finger tips

b. Cupping

## c. Fists

For each of these, make sure your wrists are supple and pretend that you are playing the drums. The movement should not end on the horse's body. It should end UP. This may be performed over any large muscle but don't do it over bone as this will hurt.

## 9. Open roll

This begins in the middle of the horse's back. Place your arms together, palms facing down. Using your body weight, lean into your arms and slowly pull them apart, sliding outwards to either end of the horse's body. As you slide your arms, stretching the horse's skin, gradually turn your arms ending with the palms facing upwards (see picture). Do this several times.

## 10. Palming

This is performed over the meridians. Allow the flat of your hand to move over the meridian, whilst working from your Hara. During the course of working along the meridian, there may be areas that you wish to linger on before moving on – this is fine, just stay in your Hara until you feel that you may move on.

## 11. Thumbing/finger pressure

This accompanies palming and is specifically done over meridian points. Use either your thumb or a finger over a point. Lean into this point and then pull back a little so that you are not in too deep. Make sure you are using your Hara and not muscle power. Listen to the horse and stay here as long as you wish or until the horse indicates you should stop.

## 12. Leg rotations

These are very small movements that echo through the body, moving any muscle that is in the way. Because it is such a small movement, the horse will allow it. This movement has great benefit to any tight muscles. It also helps with balance and is a good precursor to backing your horse.

Facing the horse's tail, lift a leg and hold it at the fetlock and hoof. Rest your outside elbow on your outside knee to support your back. Now, by rotating your ankles in a circular movement, your body will automatically rotate the hoof. (DO NOT use your arms to perform this.) Circle both to the left and to the right and then in a figure of eight. Look along the horse's back and see if you can see any evidence of this small movement.

### 13. Stretching

This is performed not only on the legs but anywhere on the horse's body. Wherever a meridian lies you may stretch the overlying skin and as a result the muscles of that particular meridian. With the legs you will be asking the limb to stretch a little further than it is accustomed. Remember you are the facilitator – do not actually pull the leg. Hold the leg in the position you want and, by lowering your bottom and stroking the leg, suggest to the horse that you want him to move his leg in a certain direction (see picture above). DO NOT over-estimate what the horse can do. Do not pull the leg. Start off small and increase gradually when you know the horse better. Cold muscles are unable to fully stretch.

### Abduct

This is a term used to describe a stretch wherein a limb is moved away from the body and away from the midline. (Remember, if someone is abducted they are taken away.)

### Adduct

This term is used to describe a stretch wherein a limb is coming in towards the body and towards or across the midline. (Remember ADD one leg and one leg and you get two.)

## The Benefits of Leg Rotations

Purpose
- To move muscles
- To move joints
- To aid relief of stiffness
- To prepare area before stretching
- To help with balance
- As a diagnostic tool
- To stimulate the meridians

When should leg rotations be used?
- Before and after exercise
- Before and after working a meridian

- Incorporated with general horse management (when picking out feet for example)
- As an introduction to bodywork for a new horse

How to change the performance of leg rotations
They can be:
- Higher or lower
- Larger or smaller
- Slower or faster
- Less or more
- Further in front or behind

# Giving a Shiatsu treatment

When preparing yourself to give Shiatsu take a few moments to check that your personal cleanliness and appearance are in order. Are your hands and fingernails clean and your nails not too long? Will your hair get in the way? Are you wearing suitable protective and comfortable clothing? Make sure that you are dressed in something you can move around in easily and that you are wearing protective footwear.

Your first step is to make yourself aware of your horse's natural movement. Ask a colleague to walk and trot him in hand and watch carefully. Make a note of any stiffness, shortness of stride or irregularity of gait.

*There are many ways in which your horse will be able to let you know whether or not he is enjoying his treatment.*

Now position your horse in the area you have decided upon for your massage. Once your horse is settled take two minutes to contemplate the massage you are about to give. Introduce yourself to your horse by standing still to one side and allow your horse to become aware of you. Take a good look at him. What attracts your attention? Hold on to this thought. Now, slow your breathing down. You will often find that it unifies with that of the horse.

Focussing on your Hara, approach your horse and place one hand on his chest and the other on his withers. Using your senses of sight, hearing, smell and touch, stand and 'listen' and tune in to what is going on under your hands. Keep your mind empty and receptive.

Step 1

Feel the horse's breathing and compare it to your own. Is it slower or faster? As you move your hands, feel for muscle tone and temperature. When and where does he appear to relax or become agitated? Does he begin to move around more or less? Try to commit these feelings to memory as you will want to compare them to the way your horse feels at the end of your session. Keep your initial contact gentle and reassuring. Now plan a treatment outline in your mind. Proceed with that treatment and allow your intuition and your hands to guide you. Be prepared to change your initial plan as necessary during the treatment.

**As you work through the massage ask yourself the following:**
- Do I need to change the pressure I'm using?
- Have I touched a sensitive area?
- Is my horse responding to the treatment?
- Is my horse getting bored or irritated?
- Has my horse yawned yet or given any indication that the treatment is working?

## A Basic treatment

### Step 1: The body sweep

Conduct a body sweep from poll to tail. This becomes a signal of commencement of treatment and helps the practitioner to connect with the horse's body. Start at the poll on the near side. Run your hands along the full length of your horse's body, noting any differences in temperature, hair and muscle texture or muscle tension. This will give you an idea of where your horse likes to be touched. He will move into you if he likes what you are doing and away from you if he doesn't. Repeat the sweep on the off side.

## Step 2: Energising

This will stimulate nerve endings and helps to move energy around the body. Working either side of the spine perform hand-over-hand energising sweeps. You can extend this all over the body if you feel the horse would benefit.

Step 2

## Step 3: Butterfly movements

These continue the work begun by the energy sweeps. Work along the same lines using the butterfly movement.

Step 3

## Step 4: Sweeping the joints

To stimulate circulation around the joints and make contact with the many acupoints in this region, make a joint sweep of the knees, hocks and fetlocks, sweeping your hands around the joints several times.

## Step 5: Body rock

This technique allows you to notice any stiff areas that will not move as easily as their counterparts. You may find that you lose your rhythm or even come to a total stop. This suggests problem areas. Commencing on the near side, body rock along the spine using one or both hands. Stand with your

Step 4

Step 5

Step 6

Step 7

hips shoulder width apart and knees soft. Once again, start at the withers placing both hands either side of the spine. Now begin to rock your body, using your momentum to move your horse. Next, holding the top of the dock, continue the rock and finish on a hair glide. Repeat on the off side.

### Step 6: Percussion

This is especially good for dispersing Jitsu. Before you begin this movement take a look at your horse's pastern and establish how long half the circumference is – this is the equivalent of 1.5 cun. This will form a measurement hereafter referred to as 1.5 cun. Using first your fingers, and then the flat of your hand, make percussion movements down the spine to the rump. Begin at the withers on whatever side of your horse's body feels appropriate. Gently and firmly percuss all the way along the muscle 1.5 cun away from the top of his spine. Keep your wrists loose and repeat two or three times on both sides. If your horse enjoys the movement make a fist of your hand and repeat.

### Step 7: Open roll

This action helps to open and stretch the back muscles and those around the shoulder and pelvic girdle. Stand with your feet placed wider apart than your hips and your arms resting on your horse's body, just below his spine with your palms facing down. Be aware of the movement coming from the hara and gently roll your arms apart ending with your palms facing upwards, gently stretching the skin beneath your arms as you go. Allow your arms to slide down and off the horse at the end of each stretch. Repeat on both sides across the spine and flanks.

## Step 8: Working the meridians
In the early stages, we work the Bladder Meridian for two reasons:
1. It is practical as this is the easiest meridian to get to know as it is presented in a straight line and is near the topline of the horse.
2. This meridian connects to every organ, affecting the entire system.

   Now, stand on the near side of your horse with the fingers of your left hand on top of his withers and the heel of your left hand resting where it falls. This is the 'mother' hand and acts as a stabiliser and comforter, helping your horse to relax. Place your right hand (the moving hand) next to your left with your fingertips near the spine. The heel of this hand should rest on your horse, 1.5 cun from his spine. Keep your mother hand still. Now move your right hand towards his tail, leaning your body weight into the heel of the right hand in a step-by-step fashion, until you reach the dock. Move from your ankles. Don't push from your shoulders. Clear your mind of anything other than the needs of your horse. Repeat this movement two or three times on both sides of your horse's body and swap the role of each hand as you swap sides. Spend as long as you

wish on any point, allowing your hand to rest in a slow holding movement over a certain spot. Let your intuition be your guide.

## Step 9: Crest rock
Stagnant energy builds up in the neck area as a result of stiffness, incorrect head carriage, bad riding and bad hoof trimming. The crest rock will help to release this. Holding the crest with one or both hands, use your fingertips to rock it to and fro. Pay careful attention to your horse's reaction and do not proceed if he is unhappy with this movement. Now, following the direction of the hair, stroke and smooth the skin from poll to shoulder. If necessary, place your other hand on the other side of the neck as a sta-

Step 9

biliser. Start gently and you may find that you can increase the movement as your horse becomes accustomed to the sensation.

### Step 10: Leg rotations

These will promote the free-flow of energy, reducing stiffness in the shoulders. Stand with your feet slightly wider than your hips at a 45 degree angle, facing the rear of the horse and ask for the foot to be picked up. Hold the foot at the fetlock joint with your inside hand over the joint in the case of the front legs and under the joint for the back (see picture). (NB: Be careful to hold the foot correctly and not have your arm in the kick-plane.) Keep the fetlock joint straight and create a circular movement from your ankles, drawing a flat circle parallel to the ground with your horse's toe. Circle the foot in each direction as many times as you feel your horse needs. Then try describing a figure of eight. Start off with tiny circles, barely moving the foot and increase the size gently as your horse allows. Some horses may find balancing through this movement difficult. Some may even find it too uncomfortable, SO GO GENTLY.

### Step 11: Gums

As your horse's gums are covered with a mucous membrane, wet your fingers to gently slip your index finger onto your horse's gums under his top lip and rub from side to side with gentle/medium even pressure. By stimulating the gums in this way you can affect the limbic system which governs the emotions, metabolic function, motivation and intuition, helping your horse to become calm and allowing healing, both physical and emotional. The acupoints within this area also help balance energy.

Step 10

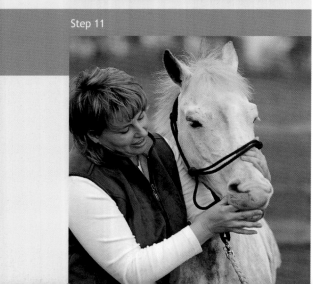
Step 11

## Step 12: Ear rub

There are many acupuncture points in the ears and by working them you can stimulate the whole body. Try using the ears to calm an anxious, fractious or nervous horse or to soothe one that is ill. Start by gently working the base of the ear with your thumb and first finger. Hold the headcollar with the other hand to keep the head steady. With your thumb on the inside of the ear and your fingers on the outside, gently pull your hand upwards, allowing the fingers to slip over the flute of the ear until you get to the tip. Here, pause for several seconds, or indeed minutes with some horses, and gently rub the tip between thumb and index finger. At the tip, there is an anti-stress point that can calm an agitated or injured horse.

Step 12

## Step 13: The tail glide

Stand to one side of your horse. Take his tail in your hands and gently pull down along the length of the tail hair. This is known as a tail glide. If you know your horse well and it is safe to do so, stand behind him (otherwise stand to the side) and take hold of the dock. Using your body for momentum, and moving from your ankles, holding the dock with both hands, gently move the dock from side to side and then around in a small circle, in a clockwise and then an anti-clockwise direction. If your horse clamps his tail down, tickle the side or the underneath of the dock to ask him to relax. If the tail remains clamped down, move on.

Working down the dock, and holding above and below each vertebra, gently wiggle the joints of the tail from side to side and then up and down all the way down to the tip. To finish, hold the dock with both hands and gently lean backwards (do not pull the tail). Wait for your horse to lean away from you, thus stretching his own spine from poll to dock. Hold this position for 30 seconds, then slowly stand up, gradually releasing the pull. Your horse may sigh or yawn – signs that he has enjoyed his massage and that energy has begun to move.

Step 13

## Step 14: Final Body Sweep

Repeat Step 1 and end your treatment holding your horse in the same way as you did at the beginning. Make a mental note of any differences that you notice. After a quiet moment or two, walk away, leaving your horse to doze.

Close off the treatment for yourself (see After the Treatment, page 18).

## Treating the meridians

Once you are more comfortable with the basic Shiatsu treatment you will begin to sense where Kyo and Jitsu appear along the Bladder Meridian. As you become more experienced, they will give you some idea of further meridians that may need treating.

To give a more advanced treatment, between steps 8 and 9, using thumb pressure and your Hara, work down the Bladder Meridian paying particular attention to the quality of the resistance that you feel under your thumb. If it is Kyo you will find that your thumb may feel as though it is disappearing down a cold hole and you will want to stay here for quite a while. If it is Jitsu it will push you away and the horse may find some discomfort. In the same way, find the meridian that is most Jitsu – you will work this with percussion, stretch and a faster step-by-step hand movement (see Step 8) that you would not use with the Kyo areas.

Now continue with your basic massage.

## Remember

- **Be relaxed**
  make no effort, don't 'do' anything
- **Always use your Hara**
  this will keep you balanced and your movements easy. Keep your posture grounded and stable
- **Regulate your breathing**
  exhale as you apply pressure
- **Don't rush**
  be calm and sensitive
- **Don't use force**
  you should never have to use pressure and if the horse is unwilling, accept this and retreat
- **Use your common sense**
  think about any given situation
- **Have an empty mind**
  be open to everything relating to the horse
- **Be non-judgemental**
  see strengths as well as weaknesses
- **Be compassionate**
  nurture your caring qualities whilst giving Shiatsu.
- **Concentrate**
  be here NOW for the horse
- **Listen to your horse**
  use all your diagnostic skills to receive information

- Use two hands

  maintain continuity of contact and always use this supporting approach to feel the energy move

- Know your limitations

  if in doubt, refer your horse to someone with more experience

- Don't be arrogant

- Develop your intuition

  trust your own feelings

- Don't break contact

  keep your treatment flowing

- Use bodyweight, not muscle

- Be modest

  have no expectations and you'll receive no disappointments

- Employ economy of movement

  act neatly and purposefully

- Visualise light (Chi)

  you may find this useful

- Be generous

  give Shiatsu joyfully and gratefully

- Be positive

  don't bring troubled or negative thoughts into a treatment

- Be aware you are not giving medical treatment

- Acknowledge your results

  be prepared that the horse may react as healing occurs and the body adjusts

# Your horse's assessment form

Create your own assessment form using this as a guide.

1. Background information
   Name:
   Height:                    Sex:
   Breed:                     Age:

   Turnout situation:    Time
                         Companions
                         Conditions
                         Rugs
   Feed:

2. Relevant history:

3. Medical history:

4. Treatment assessment
   Date:
   Any problems to be addressed?

5. Visual observations
   Appearance:

   Stationary:

   Walk:

   Trot:

   Under saddle:

6. Hands-on scan
   Muscle tone:

   Muscle tension:

   Coat texture:

   Temperature:

   Points of soreness:

5. Shiatsu given

6. Five Element diagnosis

7. Conclusion

# Part 2

# The paths to
# understanding

This book is intended as a practical every-day guide, empowering the equine enthusiast to enable his or her horse to experience Shiatsu. The reader therefore needs only a cursory understanding of the philosophy of Shiatsu as to study this in-depth takes much time. What follows is a basic introduction. However as I have said previously, once the benefits become apparent, the desire to know more usually follows.

## The beginning: Chi

Traditional Chinese philosophy propounded the belief that everything was composed of energy (Chi) in varying degrees of vibration and composition (not dissimilar to the modern belief in the atom). In an ideal state, this Chi flows in balance throughout the universe. However three principal fac-

tors can cause imbalance in Chi in the body:
- internal or emotional factors
- external or climatic factors
- lifestyle factors

Chi flows through the body via the meridian lines on which blockages can manifest themselves either as a high concentration of energy (Jitsu) or a low concentration of energy (Kyo). It is this imbalance in Chi that Shiatsu seeks to redress.

# Yin and Yang:
# Two halves of the whole

I am sure that many of you are familiar with the black and white symbol of Yin and Yang. You can find it not only in learned ancient texts but also on everyday items such as earrings, bracelets, and fabric. Yin and Yang are generally understood to be complimentary and mutually dependent opposites. In order for one to function correctly the other must be functioning optimally. For everything there is a direct opposite, for darkness there is light, where there is life there is death and so on. All Chi breaks down into Yin and Yang and Yin and Yang are states of being rather than absolutes. Each contains a seed of the other and nothing is totally either Yin or Yang. They can also change into each other. The most quoted example is this: The water in a

lake (Yin) is heated by the sun during the day and transformed into vapour (Yang). At night, when the air cools, this vapour condenses and becomes water once again.

From this you will see that Yang symbolises the more immaterial and rarefied states of matter and Yin symbolises the more material and dense states. They both also have certain qualities that have become attributed to them over the centuries:

| YIN | YANG |
|---|---|
| Darkness | Light |
| Moon | Sun |
| Shade | Brightness |
| Rest | Activity |
| Cold | Hot |
| Inside | Outside |
| Earth | Heaven |
| Female | Male |
| Wet | Dry |
| Soft | Hard |
| Pliable | Solid |
| Contraction | Expansion |
| Inward looking | Outgoing |
| Sinking | Rising |
| Downward | Upward |
| Lazy | Overactive |
| Lethargic | Unsettled |

However this is all relative and moveable. A noisy classroom that we would call Yang is in fact Yin compared to a jet aircraft taking off. However compared to a library it is indeed Yang. So knowledge of the comparison helps ascertain the right answer. Try the following exercise to help you understand Yin and Yang.

Are the following Yin or Yang? And how might they transform from one to the other?

EXAMPLE: A cup of hot tea. This is predominantly Yang in nature (as it is hot). Leave it to cool to room temperature for half an hour and it would become predominantly Yin in nature (as it gets colder).

1. A sherbet lemon sweet compared to a boiled sweet
2. A stationary bus compared to a moving bus
3. A block of ice compared to water
4. A thumping migraine headache compared to no headache
5. A footballer lining up a goal shot compared to a footballer kicking the ball
6. An aeroplane taking off compared to one sitting on the runway
7. The Prime Minister delivering a speech compared to all the Commons shouting
8. A soft boiled egg compared to a hard boiled egg
9. A rowdy football match compared to a bowls competition
10. A heavy rock CD when being played compared to one sitting on the shelf
11. A runner at the beginning of a marathon compared to a runner in the middle of his race
12. A lorry that has run out of petrol compared to one with a full tank
13. A book on a shelf compared to one being read
14. A cold winter's day compared to a hot summer's day
15. A sneeze compared to a yawn
16. Your thought process at the minute
17. A horse that has laminitis compared to one that does not
18. A saddle that is too tight compared to one that fits
19. A horse who needs the dentist compared to a horse just having had the dentist
20. A horse in a stable on its own compared to one out in the field with companions
21. A rearing horse compared to a quiet horse with all four feet on the ground
22. A horse in the collecting ring compared to one that is competing
23. A horse with colic compared to feeling well
24. A cross country competition compared to dressage
25. A horse at feed time in his stable compared to a horse standing in a stable doing nothing

## Answers
1. Yang as there is an explosion of sherbet on the tongue
2. Yin because it is still
3. Yang as it is more solid
4. Yang due to the pain and the heat
5. Yin as the ball is static
6. Yang due to the noise and energy given off
7. Yin as the Prime Minister is less noisy!!
8. Yin as the egg is soft and not hard

9. Yang as the match is more noisy and active
10. Yang as the sound is loud
11. Yin as there is no activity yet and the runner's temperature is cool
12. Yin as there is no activity and the tank is empty
13. Yin as there is no activity. But a book on karate could be seen as being more Yang compared to one on meditation!
14. Yin as it is cold
15. Yang as it is more active
16. You decide!
17. Yang as there is pain and destruction
18. Yang as the badly fitting saddle will be causing pain
19. Yang if there are tooth issues and because someone is going into the horse's mouth
20. Yin as there is very little movement
21. Yang as more activity
22. Yin as there is less activity and emotion
23. Yang as there is pain and distress
24. Yang as cross country is more physically active than dressage
25. Yang as there is more activity

Now consider your horse:

His belly, inside his legs and under his tail are all Yin.

His back, outside of legs and surface of tail will all be Yang.

The organs in the body are described as either Yin or Yang depending how solid the organs are;

Yin organs: liver, heart, lungs, kidney and spleen

Yang organs: gall bladder, small intestine, large intestine, stomach, bladder. The persona and physical characteristics of your horse can be summed up as Yin or Yang:

| YIN | YANG |
|---|---|
| Quiet | Extrovert |
| Conformational problems | More physical/ built for action |
| Spooky | Brave |
| Continually breaks down | Never ill |

But of course you could have a horse that has never previously been ill but catches strangles - there are no absolutes.

# The Five Elements

Chi is therefore divided into Yin and Yang, but it can be further defined and classified by what is known as The Five Elements (although 'elements' is not a true translation and 'transformation' or 'phase' would be closer to the original oriental terminology). This is a method of symbolisation that Western society generally finds easier to understand than the more abstract Yin and Yang. The ancient Japanese and Chinese revered the Five Elements: Earth, Metal, Water, Wood and Fire. To each were attributed qualities and characteristics based on common energies and these were then used to help understand the interactive play of Chi in their everyday lives.

In Oriental medicine they were used as a method of diagnosis and it is this method we use in this book.

In the same way that Chi is at the core of everything, these Five Elements combine to make up the whole. Visually this tends to be represented as a wheel that is known as the Shen or creative cycle and shows how one element feeds into, and is fed by, another and how each element exercises control on its opposite number – the Ko cycle. More of this later.

As previously said, each meridian is related to certain organs, it also assumes the characteristics of one of the Five Elements:

Wood = The Liver and Gall Bladder Meridians
Fire = The Small Intestine and Heart Meridians
Plus the Triple Heater and Heart Protector Meridians
Earth = The Stomach and Spleen Meridians
Metal = The Lung and Large Intestine Meridians
Water = The Kidney and Bladder Meridians

Each element contains
a Yin and a Yang meridian

Wood = The Liver (Yin) and Gall Bladder (Yang) Meridians
Fire = The Heart Yin) and Small Intestine (Yang) Meridians
Plus the Heart Protector (Yin) and Triple Heater (Yang) Meridians

Earth = The Spleen (Yin) and Stomach (Yang) Meridians
Metal = The Lung (Yin) and Large Intestine (Yang) Meridians
Water = The Kidney (Yin) and Bladder (Yang) Meridians

The Elements can also determine the character and physical type of your horse and what ailments he may be susceptible to. Once you have a good working knowledge of the characteristics of each Element, you will find it therefore follows which meridian your horse needs you to treat.

### The Shen cycle

- Wood creates Fire – the burning of Wood
- Fire enriches Earth – through ashes
- Earth contains Metal – the most precious metal being gold
- Metal condenses Water
- Water feeds Wood – the trees

This is the Shen or creative cycle that draws energy through the elements and helps balance the whole system. If there is an imbalance in one element it will have a knock on effect on the others around the circle. This is known as the Law of Mother-Child.

If the meridian you want to work (say the Bladder) is lacking in energy you would work the preceding element (Metal), the Mother element, to boost the energy that could then be passed on. However

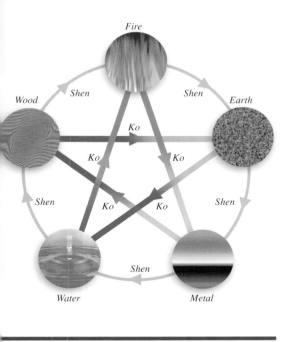

*Fire*

*Shen*

*Shen*

*Earth*

*Wood*

*Ko*

*Ko*

*Ko*

*Shen*

*Ko*

*Ko*

*Shen*

*Shen*

*Water*

*Metal*

*The Shen cycle circulates energy from one element to another; the Ko cycle is the control cycle and keeps the elements in the Shen cycle in check.*

### The Ko Cycle

- Wood penetrates the Earth - roots that bind the Earth
- Earth limits the flow of Water - think of a river bank dictating its flow
- Water extinguishes Fire
- Fire melts Metal
- Metal cuts Wood

For example, if your horse becomes over-excited (Fire) you would look at it as the kidneys (Water) becoming weak and not having enough energy to put the fire out. Or if he became very spooky (Bladder Meridian) the energy in the Earth Element was not able to bolster the Bladder Meridian and keep it in check.

By utilising Five Element theory not only will you be able to identify what meridians you need to work to keep your horse in optimum health but you will also be able to ascertain what type of horse you have and whether you, his owner, are compatible with him.

if the meridian you are wanting to work (Bladder) is overfull of energy you could also work the next element along (Wood), the Child element, to draw the energy through.

The elements within the Shen cycle would continue in their creative activities ad infinitum were they not kept in check in some way. This task is performed by a control cycle, the Ko cycle. In diagrams it is depicted by the star shape within the Shen cycle. The Ko cycle also allows harmony to be restored to an element that, when weak, cannot perform its task of controlling its opposed element, or becomes so full of energy that it over powers its opposed element.

### How to use the Five Elements theory to help your horse

On our creative wheel (over page) are aligned various correspondences (or characteristics) to help you discover which meridians you need to work in order to help your horse.

Here are a few examples that will help you read the wheel. REMEMBER you cannot harm your horse by working the wrong meridian. However, if you are working the wrong meridian your horse will tell you so

Part 2

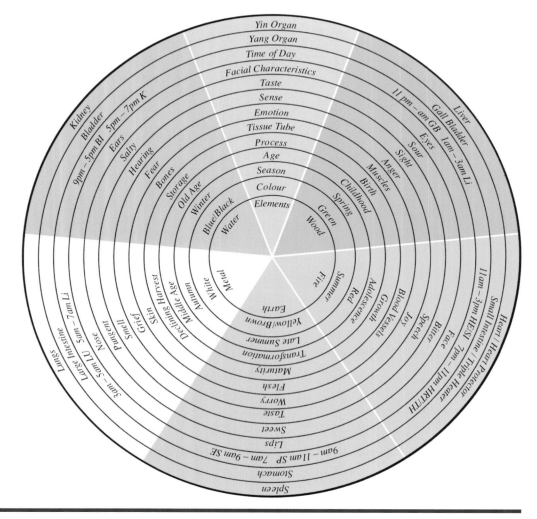

*The creativ wheel: each element has particular characteristics that can be used not only to help identify which meridian needs work, but also to help you understand your horse.*

by moving away, swishing his tail or by showing any of the other negative signs that we have discussed earlier on in this book.

1. If you have a horse that is spooky and jumps at any little thing he will probably have a Water imbalance so the meridians you would work are Bladder and Kidney. The Bladder is easy to work and is in contact with all the other meridians. The Kidney

is a little more awkward as the point where the meridian commences is in between the bulbs of the heels and you may not want to start there especially if your horse is jumping about! So initially start your work further up the meridian.

2. You may have a horse that has digestive problems, diarrhoea or colics often. From the wheel you would look at working the

Metal Element (Large Intestine) or the Fire Element (Small Intestine) you could also try the Earth Element (Stomach and Spleen) if you feel that the issue stems from the stomach.

To help you decide which you would go for you would look at the other characteristics that go with each element. For instance you would opt for the Metal Meridian if your horse was middle aged and had a skin problem BUT you would choose the Fire Meridians if your horse was in adolescence, made a lot of vocal noises and had issues with his blood vessels.

If, however, your horse has got over adolescence, is settling down to life and is a worrier with issues with the flesh you would look at the Stomach and Spleen Meridians of the Earth Element.

3. Your horse may be very angular and often has problems with his muscles, either strained, pulled or painful, in this case look at working the Wood Element (Liver and Gall Bladder Meridians)

You may find that on looking at the Five Elements your horse falls into one or more of these categories. In this case you can either

a) see which meridian has least energy by using your touch skills; or

b) use additional methods known as Yu points, Tings or Zones to help determine which is the correct meridian to work (see page 42).

## The effects of Yin and Yang on the Five Elements

However, Yin and Yang and the Five Elements do not stand alone, they are part of each other and affect each other. For example, when looking at the energy of a particular Yang meridian we must be aware that the meridian could be too Yang and therefore display characteristics of excess. The Gall Bladder Meridian in excess would show in the horse's behaviour as imminent explosion, tight jaw, and impatience. The same Yang meridian on another occasion could be lacking in sufficient energy to bring it to its optimum and therefore will be considered depleted, showing different traits. Taking the Gall Bladder Meridian as an example, once again, this lack of energy will present itself in the horse as displays of lack of vigour, joint stiffness, depression and timidity. The same can apply to a Yin meridian.

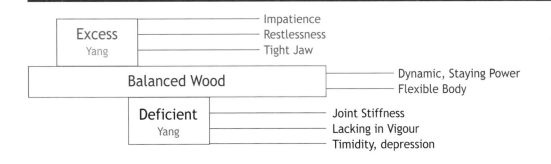

*Yu Points
(Traditional Chinese
Association Points)*

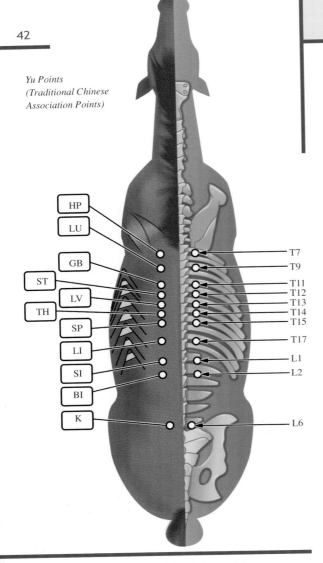

HP
LU
GB
ST
LV
TH
SP
LI
SI
BI
K

T7
T9
T11
T12
T13
T14
T15
T17
L1
L2
L6

*The Yu points are situated in the intercostal
spaces between the ribs.*

## Yu points

Yu points are positioned along the Bladder
Meridian and are specific sites associated
with individual organs. They lie in the gaps
between vertebrae where you can feel them
by thumb pressure. They will be noticed by
the tenderness of each of the spots. They tend
to indicate long-standing problems with the

energy of the individual organs rather than
the day-to-day fluctuation of energy running
through the meridians. You can use the Yu
points to treat or to determine which meridian is in the most in need of work. Each Yu
point is situated in the region where the en-
ervation for the local area exits the spine. For
example, the lung Yu point will be located
near the exiting nerve that services the lungs.

The best way to know where the Yu points
lie is to learn them by rote. In the classes that
I teach we use mnemonics to help us remember. Here's an example:

Horses
Love
Getting lots of
Sugar
Lumps
To
Show
Life
Should
Be
Kind

## Tings points

These are another way of deciding where
your treatment is going to start. Each meridian ends or begins at a Ting point just above
the coronet band and Shiatsu practitioners use
these as a diagnostic tool. When stimulated,
they have incredible healing abilities. These
Ting points remain the same all the time.

The Ting point relates to the quality of the energy in the organ as opposed to the quality of the energy running through the meridian.

How do I use the Tings
to determine which meridian I work?
Use your thumb or finger to work around the coronet band being mindful which point feels the most Kyo and which the most Jitsu. Determine this firstly on the forelegs and then on the hind. Then compare the fore and hind legs and decide which is most Kyo and which most Jitsu. Now start your treatment by working the meridian that is the most Kyo. You can then go and work the meridian relating to the organ which shows the most Kyo and then the meridian relating to the organ which shows the most Jitsu.

How do I know where each Ting point lies?
I find that the following mnemonic helps my students to remember where the Ting points lie:

Foreleg
(Starting at the front mid toe point, working around the hoof via the inside, centre back and outside.)

    Three – (Triple Heater)
    Little – (Large Intestine)
    Lumps – (Lungs)
    Happen – (Heart Protector)
    Hot – (Heart)
    Sadly – (Small Intestine)

*These photos and those on the next page show the meridian points that are also Ting points. If you haven't time for a full treatment stimulating the Ting points can do a graet deal of good.*

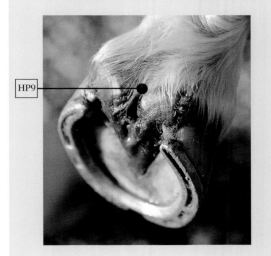

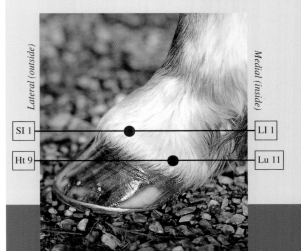

St 45

K 1

Lateral (outside)

GB 44

Bl 67

Medial (inside)

Li 1

Sp 1

### Hind leg

(Starting at the front mid toe point, working around the hoof via the inside, centre back and outside.)

Stop - (Stomach)
Lively - (Liver)
Sportsmen - (Spleen)
Kissing - (Kidney)
Blonde - (Bladder)
Gadabouts -(Gall Bladder)

## Zones

Zones are areas on the horse's back that help you to choose which meridian you need to work and, like the Yu points, they are in the areas appertaining to the nerves that exit the spinal column to service certain areas of the body. There has not been a lot of research into Zones so you may find that as you become more experienced you identify the areas in slightly different places.

The Zones relate to the quality of the energy that runs through the meridians as opposed to the quality of energy in the organs.

### How do I use the Zones to determine which meridian I work?

Place your flattened hand on the Zone area and again determine whether you have an area that is Kyo or Jitsu earlier. Make a mental note of your conclusion. Work your hands over each Zone and determine which merid-

ians most needs attention. Remember the
empty, cold Kyo meridian is the first that
you should work.

How do I know where the Zones are?
These will also have to be learned by rote.

Starting on the nearside of the horse:
    Speedy (Stomach)
    Stallions (Spleen)
    Love (Large Intestine)
    Shiatsu (Small Intestine)

Farside of the horse
    Let (Lungs)
    Happy (Heart Protector)
    Horses (Heart)
    Liberally (Liver)
    Graze (Gall Bladder)
    Though (Triple Heater)
    Bucking (Bladder)
    Kicking (Kidney)
    Blatantly (Bladder)

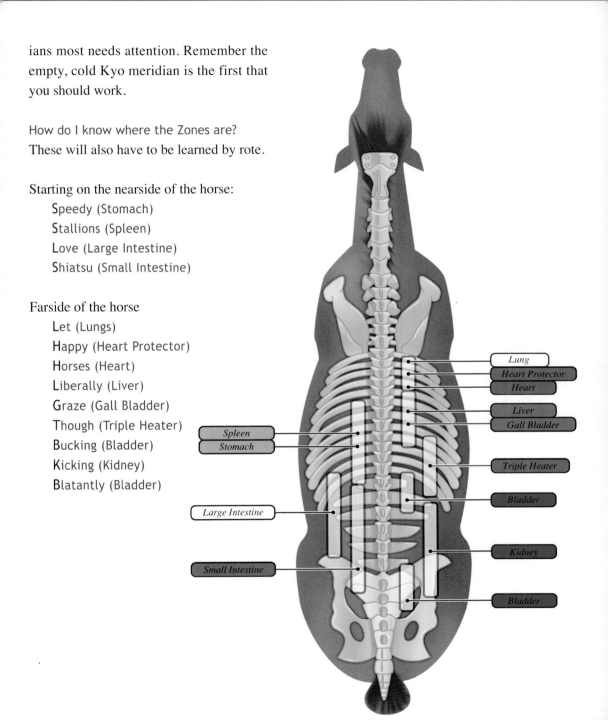

*The Zones are another way of determining which meridian to treat.*

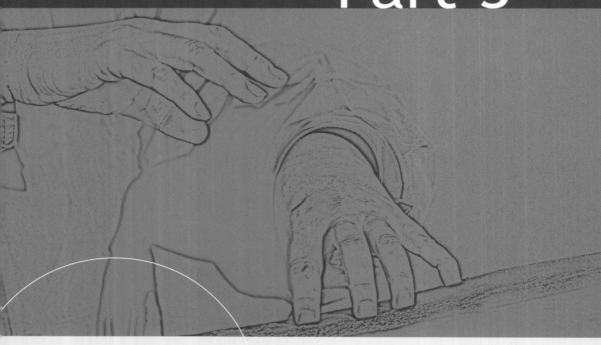

# Part 3

# An introduction to the meridians via the Five Elements

In the early stages of understanding and working with Shiatsu, most students find the Five Elements the most comfortable method of attributing characteristics to a subject. As we have already said, the elements also determine the character and physical type of your horse and where his physical weaknesses and strengths may lie. Once you have a good working knowledge of the characteristics of each element, you will find it therefore follows which merid-

ian your horse needs you to treat. Both the characteristics of the element and the signs of balance and imbalance can also be used to help you understand your horse on a daily basis.

In Part 3 we look at:
- The characteristics (or correspondences) of each element
- How to recognise which element best represents your horse at any given time

- The meridians governed by each element and the key treatment points on those meridians
- Relevant anatomical information looking at key organs, muscles, bones and bodily functions

## Stretching exercises

Relevant stretching exercises are also included with each element appropriate to the meridians governed by that element. Stretching is an integral part of a Shiatsu treatment. It not only increases the blood flow throughout the body but also aids the movement of good quality energy through interconnected meridians. One stretch can therefore have quite an effect on many points, helping to dissipate Jitsu and ease aching joints. Stretching exercises can be performed at the beginning and again at the end of a treatment to measure results. Remember, however, cold muscles don't necessarily stretch as well as warm muscles.

# The Wood Element

Governing the Liver
and Gall Bladder Meridians

Whilst it would appear that Wood, synonymous with spring and new growth, begins the creative cycle, it must be remembered that this is a cycle and that the new growth and feeling of optimism of this element is fed and nourished by Water. Wood energy is rising and expanding energy, bursting with activity. It is a youthful element, associated with the colour green, and in its inexperience sometimes prone to outbursts and expressions of anger and extreme emotion. All this energy is channelled to create and feed the Fire element. Wood's enthusiasm controls and uplifts the gravity of Earth and in turn its exuberance is contained by Metal.

The characteristics of the element and the signs of balance and imbalance can be used as indications of direction towards the appropriate meridians for treatment and also as tools to help you understand your horse on a daily basis.

## Characteristics of the Wood Element

| | |
|---|---|
| Season: | Spring |
| Time of day: | Early morning |
| Energy quality: | Upward, rising energy |
| Colour: | Yellow/green |
| Smell: | Rancid |
| Taste: | Sour |
| Sense: | Sight |
| High Tide Time: | 11pm – 3am<br>(Gall Bladder 11pm – 1am/liver 1am – 3am) |
| Emotion: | Anger |
| Voice tone: | Barking/shouting |
| Tissue: | Joints |
| Concepts: | Flexibility, adaptability, resolution |

## Signs of balance/imbalance

### Signs of balance
- vital and dynamic
- staying power
- flexible body

### Signs of imbalance
- about to explode
- tight head, especially the jaw
- impatient
- restless, bold, reckless
- likes to be in charge
- rigidity in movements
- lacking vigour
- joint rigidity
- depression
- timidity

## Recognising the Wood horse

### Appearance
- His strong muscular physique and good conformation are sustained by and support his natural athletic prowess.
- The Wood horse is likely to have a distinctive body odour.

### Character
- The Wood horse is the choice for any rider with strong competitive instincts as his conformation and temperament make him a natural athlete.

- He has the characteristics to make him naturally competitive, both in competition and in the field.
- He will enjoy his work and be impatient with rest.
- Unlike many horses he will express himself well in competition and activity, finding this an outlet for any tension rather than a cause of anxiety.
- This horse will have a strong will and sense of self-awareness that may cause him to be stubborn and attention seeking.
- In the field, he will probably be the alpha horse, asserting himself over his companions. He may also try to assert himself over his rider!
- In the wrong hands the Wood horse can easily be misunderstood. This usually results in his withdrawal and expressions of depression.
- Although on the whole this horse tends to get on with things, he is very sensitive to sound and light. Be aware of this when hacking out.
- He will be a favourite with the judges due to his free-moving limbs.
- Be prepared – he will be an energetic horse!

### Training
- He may express his frustration and boredom as aggression or behavioural problems – keep him busy!
- This horse responds well to challenges. Always have a goal in mind.

- Enthusiastic and keen to work, he may be inclined to emotional outburst when unsure about what is expected of him.
- The Wood horse will suit a confident rider prepared to see his forceful personality as a plus and work with him.
- In return a relationship built on mutual trust and respect will evolve with this horse.

## Health
- His naturally forceful ways may get him into trouble on occasion – watch out for field injuries.
- His enthusiasm for athletic expression makes him prone to injuries of the muscle, tendon and ligament. He could be prone to muscle spasm.
- Be careful not to overwork this willing horse as he may suffer from exhaustion.
- His hooves will require attention as they will be inclined to be dry and brittle.
- With a sensitive nature, he may be prone to skin conditions and itchiness.

## Horse/rider relationship
The Wood horse is certainly not a horse for a fearful or novice rider – best suited to this horse is a well balanced Wood rider who would understand the horse's nature and treat him with respect and sensitivity. The Wood horse in balance would also work well with the Earth rider, who would temper the demanding nature of the horse with care and evenness of hand but would also allow his creative and flexible nature to thrive.

*The Wood horse has a strong will and sense of self-awareness.*

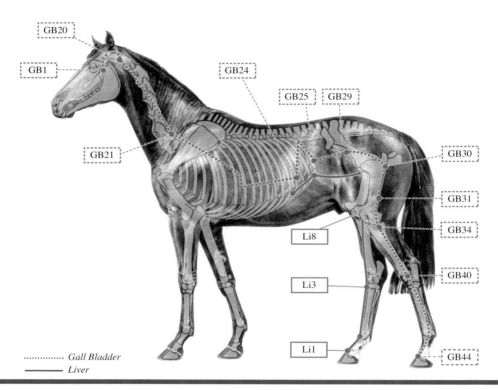

GB20
GB1
GB24
GB25
GB29
GB21
GB30
GB31
GB34
Li8
GB40
Li3
Li1
GB44

·············· *Gall Bladder*
———— *Liver*

*The Liver and Gall Bladder Meridians
are governed by the Wood Element.*

## The Wood Meridians

### The Liver Meridian

The liver meridian begins on the hind leg just above the coronet band and runs up the inside front edge of the cannon bone to the hind knuckle end of the femur. It then disappears internally, emerging at the tip of the 18th rib, ending at the 14th intercostal space, a little nigher than the elbow.

### Liver 1 (Li1)

This is a Ting point

On the inside of the hoof just above the coronet band, one third of the distance from the centre front to the centre back of the hoof.

Indications: Laminitis, sidebone, eye disorders, hoof disorders, azoturia, hepatitis, skin allergies.

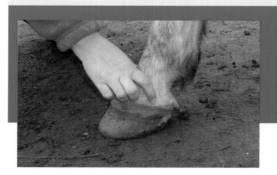

### Liver 3 (Li3)

Benefits the liver

This is found on the inside and slightly forward of the cannon bone at the level of the head of the inside splint bone.

Indications: pain in the hock, eye problems, uterine disease, convulsions.

### Liver 8 (Li8)

This is located on the inside of the femur behind the epicondyle between the gracilis and semitendinosus muscles.

Indications: pain in the inside aspect of the stifle or thigh, rear abdominal pain uterine prolapse.

### Liver 13 (Li13)

Benefits spleen and liver functions and balances the Yin organs.

This is found at the lower end of the 18th rib.

Indications: myositis, muscle soreness abdominal pain.

### Liver 14 (Li14)

Benefits liver function and smooth flow of Chi

Located in the 14th intercostal space.

Indications: hepatitis, muscle soreness.

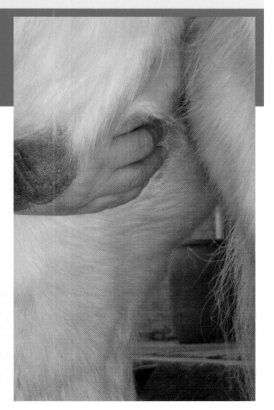

# The Gall Bladder Meridian

The Gall Bladder Meridian begins in the rear corner of the eye and then runs in between the ears to a point on the occipital condyle. It then travels down the neck to a point between the last neck and first thoracic vertebrae.

Next it travels across the shoulder blades and chest to the 15th intercostal space moving through the 18th rib, curving through the hip area and down the outside of the thigh. It then runs down the tibia, cannon bone and pastern, ending just above the coronet band, one third of the distance from the centre front to the centre back of the hoof.

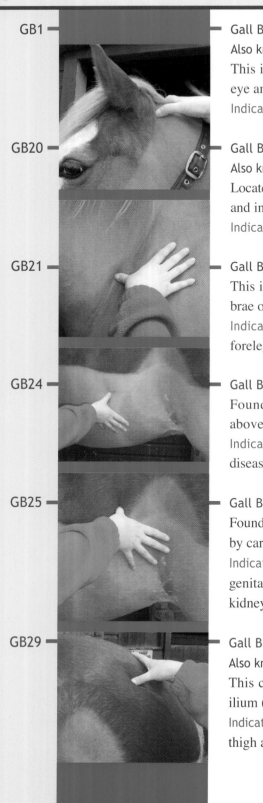

GB1

GB20

GB21

GB24

GB25

GB29

## Gall Bladder 1 (GB1)

**Also known as Tai Yang (great Yang)**

This is found 0.5 cun away from the rear corner of the eye and slightly lower.

Indications: conjunctivitis, heat-stroke, headache.

## Gall Bladder 20 (GB20)

**Also known as Feng Men (wind gate)**

Located in a depression just behind the occipital condyle, and in front of the wings of the atlas.

Indications: neck pain, wobbler syndrome, fever, cold.

## Gall Bladder 21 (GB21)

This is between the 7th cervical and 1st thoracic vertebrae over the cervical ventral serrate muscle.

Indications: neck and shoulder pain, arthritis of the foreleg.

## Gall Bladder 24 (GB24)

Found in the 14th intercostal space, just behind and above Li14.

Indications: abdominal pain, muscle soreness, liver disease.

## Gall Bladder 25 (GB25)

Found at the back edge of the 18th rib where it is joined by cartilage and the lumbar muscles.

Indications: Pain in the lumbar region, kidney and urogenital problems. Profoundly affects the balance of the kidney meridian.

## Gall Bladder 29 (GB29)

**Also known as Ju Lao (at the hip)**

This can be found in a depression half way along the ilium (half way along the pelvic bone).

Indications: rheumatism of the hind limb, myositis of the thigh and rump muscles.

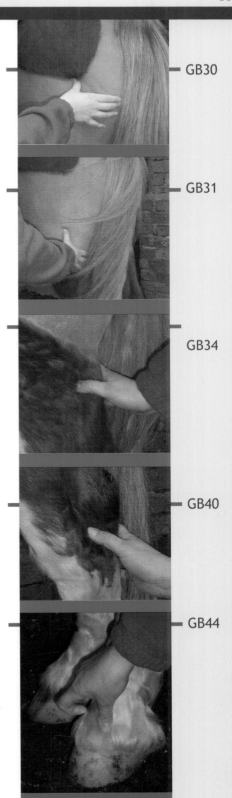

GB30

GB31

GB34

GB40

GB44

**Gall Bladder 30 (GB30)**

This is in a depression between the thigh bone and the point of buttock.

Indications: rheumatism of the hind limb, sciatica, hind limb paralysis.

**Gall Bladder 31 (GB31)**

Also known as Xiao Kua, (3rd trochanter)

This is on the back of the femur 6 cun below and rearwards from the 3rd trochanter over the muscular groove of the biceps femoris.

Indications: pain and sprain of the hip joint, pelvic infection.

**Gall Bladder 34 (GB34)**

Also known as Feng Long (flourishing)

Found in a space between the tibia and fibula, between the long and lateral digital extensor.

Indications: weakness and pain in the hind limb. Influential point for tendon, ligament, fascia and muscle conditions, muscle atrophy, weakness of the joints. Strengthens the caudal back and extremities.

**Gall Bladder 40 (GB40)**

This point is found on the front side of the tibia, lower than the lateral malleolus, overlying the tendon of the digital extensor muscle.

Indications: pain in the distal extremities.

**Gall Bladder 44 (GB44)**

This is a Ting point

Also known as Hou Ti Men, (heel of the pelvic hoof)

This lies on the outside of the hoof just above the coronet band, one third of the distance from the centre front to the centre back of the hoof.

Indications: laminitis, arthritis, hock problems.

## Stretches for the Wood Element

### Gall Bladder

1. Stand at a 45 degree angle to the back legs of the horse, facing the tail and pick the back leg up, resting your outside elbow on your outside knee. Moving from your ankles, gently circle the leg left, right and in a figure of eight.
2. Try to encourage the horse to smell his tail in order to stretch the meridian that runs along his side. If this doesn't work, use a carrot to achieve the sidewards and rearwards stretch.
3. Ask for the opposite hind foot and draw the leg towards you under the horse's body, holding Gall Bladder 40 as you take it down and across.

### Liver

1. Stand at a 45 degree angle to the back legs of the horse, facing the tail and pick the back leg up, resting your outside elbow on your outside knee. Gently circle the leg left, right and in a figure of eight.
2. Gently stretch the leg under the horse and abduct holding Li3.
3. Palm stretch between Li14 and 13. All meridians may be stretched by palming sections.

Gall Bladder 2.
Gall Bladder 3.

Gall Bladder 1.

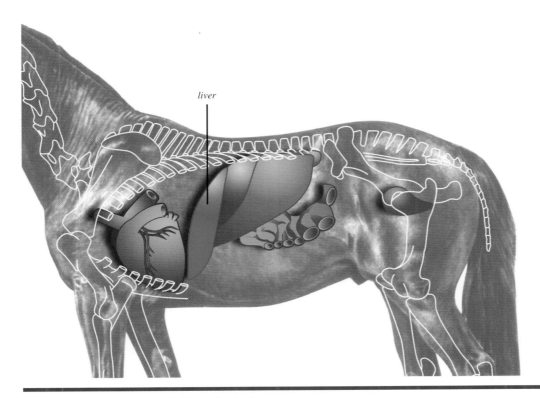

*liver*

*The liver is believed to have over 100 different functions!*

# The liver

The liver lies between the diaphragm and the stomach and is kept in place by six ligaments and the internal pressure of the abdomen. It is a crucial metabolic centre of the body. It possesses a duct (the hepatic duct) that carries bile into the duodenum as the horse does not possess a gall bladder. It is the largest of all the glands (the others being the pancreas and salivary glands) and has three lobes. It is one of the accessory glands of the diges-

tive system supplied by arteries, veins, nerves and lymph channels. It also possesses a duct that carries bile into the duodenum.

The liver and its functions are not only fed by normal blood flow but also by specific vessels – the hepatic artery and the hepatic portal vein. The hepatic artery brings oxygenated blood to the liver and the hepatic portal vein brings blood rich in nutrients from the gut to the liver.

The horse's liver weighs between 5 - 9 kg (12 - 20 lbs). It is reddish brown in colour and is covered with connective tissue.

It is thought that the liver has over 100 different functions, which can be divided into three basic types:

- Regulation of metabolism: these include proteins, carbohydrates and fats.
- Production of bile.
- Detoxification of toxic materials absorbed into the body.

These are the liver's main functions:

- Unwanted excess protein in the form of amino acids is broken down by liver cells and forms ammonia. This is then converted to a less toxic nitrogenous compound, urea, by the action of particular enzymes. Urea is then excreted via the kidneys.
- Toxins (such as drugs) that may be of harm to the horse are detoxified by absorption and chemical recomposition within the liver cells.
- Working in conjunction with the spleen, the liver cells break down old red blood cells (haemoglobin) and excrete them in the bile. This is one reason for the dark colouration of faecal matter.
- Fat or fat-like substances known as lipids are emulsified in the duodenum by bile produced by the liver cells. The liver cells also extract lipids from the blood and either break them down or change them to body fat.
- Production of bile salts.
- Excess glucose is stored in the liver to regulate the amount in circulation in the body.
- The liver acts as a storehouse for iron and vitamins A, D, and B12.

## Bile

The horse does not have a gall bladder (the organ commonly used to store bile). Instead, bile is continually trickled into the duodenum and is synthesised by liver cells, hence the horse's need to trickle feed.

Bile is green/yellow in colour that comes from the breakdown of haemoglobin. It does not contain digestive enzymes.

Bile required for the emulsification of fats in the digestive system. After they have been used in the small intestine, the bile salts sodium taurocholate and glycocholate, are actively re-absorbed into the hepatic portal vein and taken back to the liver to be reused again in the bile.

# Skeletal structure of the horse

When working with Shiatsu it is invaluable to be familiar with both the skeletal and muscular systems of the horse and it is these systems that define the equine conformation. Both the skeleton and the attachment of muscles to it dictate how the horse moves, whether he is in balance and whether or not he can perform certain manoeuvres. For the Shiatsu practitioner it is often a visual study of the static horse and his mobility that can determine an initial point of treatment. In this section we will deal with the skeleton.

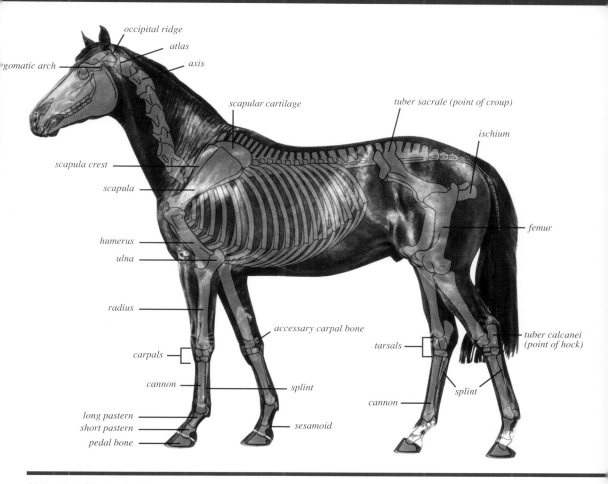

*Main points of the horse's skeleton.*

## Functions of the skeleton:

- It gives form to the body: the skeleton is a framework for other body tissues.
- It enables locomotion by providing points for muscle and ligament attachment.
- It protects the vital internal organs.
- It acts as a mineral store for calcium and phosphorous.
- It produces red and white blood cells in specific bones (eg long bones of the legs, the ribs and the breast bone).

- It has a function to perform in body language. The topline of the horse is a loud hailer to other equines (or interested parties) and is full of expression and tips on how he is feeling.

For the Shiatsu practitioner, the skeleton also provides the basis for point location that is then further directed by the overlying muscles.

## Bone structure

Bones are living tissue made up of mainly inorganic calcium salts, in the largest part calcium phosphate and calcium carbonate. Understandably the young horse (as in the human child) has more of this organic matter (on average 60% of his total bone matter) than the older horse (as little as 35%). This of course is all dependent on the horse's lifestyle and conditions of work, as well as hereditary influences. The amount of organic matter will dictate the suppleness of the bone – the more there is the more supple and less easily broken it is.

### Bone is responsive to environmental changes such as

- physical loading
- variation in blood supply
- nutrition

### The skeleton may be divided into two parts for easy referral

- **The Axial skeleton**
  This is the principal support structure of the body and includes the skull, vertebrae, sternum, ribs and hyoid bone.
- **The Appendicular skeleton**
  This includes the pectoral and pelvic girdles and the bones of fore and hind limbs

### Types of bone

- **Long bones:** The appendicular skeleton ie the legs. Each of these bones has an enlarged end known as the epiphysis that pro-vides a larger weight-bearing area less prone to dislocation.
- **Short bones:** These are often found in groups that help with shock absorbency and are the point of hock (os calcis), carpal and tarsal bones (bones in the front and hind leg respectively), sesamoids and patella.
- **Flat bones:** These help to protect underlying organs such as the cranial plates that protect the brain.
- **Irregular bones:** Any bone that does not fit into the above three categories will be classed here. For instance the bones of the pelvis and the vertebral column.

### The spine

The spine consists of an horizontal column of bony vertebrae that articulate with each other. Separating each vertebra is a cartilaginous disc that acts as a shock absorber and allows a small amount of movement, but are not as pliable as human discs and therefore do not allow the same flexibility. They also house a dense bundle of nerves – the spinal cord. There are 'service exits' for these nerves between each junction, radiating to other parts of the body.

### The functions of the spine:

1. To protect the spinal cord from damage.
2. To provide a structure for suspension and propulsion of the horse's bodyweight.
3. To provide attachment for the ribs, which protect the vital internal organs.

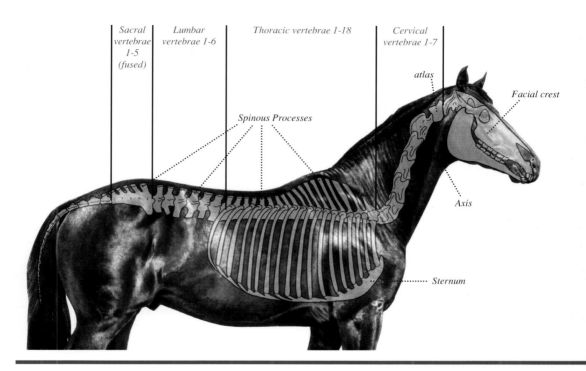

*The horse's vertebral column is separated into four sections: cervical, thoracic lumbar and sacral.*

## Different sections of the spinal column

### Cervical:

- Made up of seven bones including the atlas and axis
- Small spinous processes allow for a wide range of movement.

### Thoracic:

- Eighteen bones attached to 18 pairs of ribs.
- These have a limited movement. They bear long spinous processes that restrict upward bending.
- The first 8 pairs are true ribs, attached directly to the sternum
- The remaining 10 pairs are false ribs, attached to the sternum by means of cartilaginous extrusions.

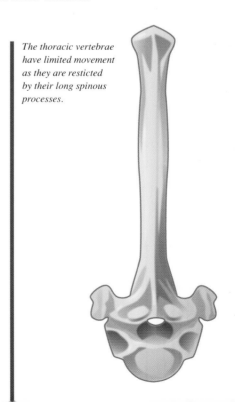

*The thoracic vertebrae have limited movement as they are resticted by their long spinous processes.*

*The lumbar vertebrae control
the forward thrust of movement.*

### Lumbar:

- Six bones.
- The forward thrust of the hind legs is transferred to the body through the lumbar vertebrae, which are large and strong and prevent lateral movement due to long lateral processes. Thus the power from the forward thrust moves the horse forward in a straight line and not sideways as happens in the spine of a snake, or upwards as in the cat.

### Sacral:

- Five bones fused together forming the sacrum.

### Coccygeal:

- Approximately 18 – 20 bones.
- These have limited use.

The horse's back has developed with evolution. The necessity to be able to relax, but at a moment's notice to be able to flee with speed and vigour has created a need for a varying degree of flexibility and rigidity. Areas of flexion need greater muscle control and it is often these areas that are vulnerable in the ridden horse eg the joint between the lumbar vertebrae and the sacrum and the sacroiliac joint between the pelvis and the spine.

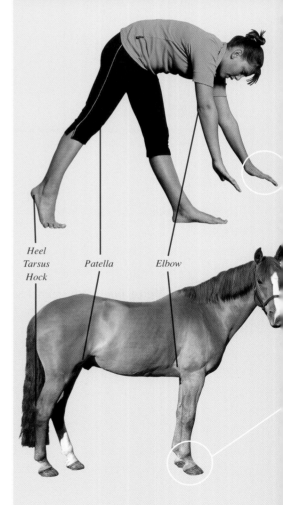

Compare the common points
in the skeleton of the human and the horse.

*Heel
Tarsus
Hock*

*Patella*

*Elbow*

It is interesting to draw comparisons between the human and equine skeletons and
the human arm and equine leg. As you can
see below there are common points.

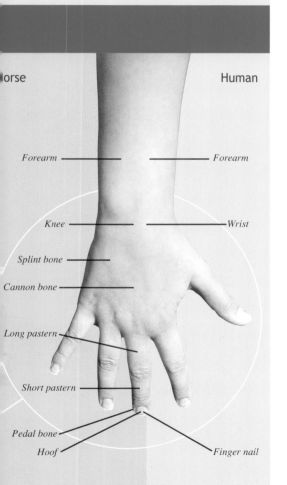

Horse                                    Human

Forearm ————————        ———————— Forearm

Knee ————————        ————————Wrist

Splint bone ————————

Cannon bone ————————

Long pastern —————

Short pastern —————

Pedal bone —————
Hoof —————                        ———— Finger nail

# The Fire Element

·

Governing the Heart,
Small Intestine,
Heart Protector
and Triple Heater Meridians

Continuing on the path of energy travel-
ling around the Shen cycle, Fire is the next
element bursting forth from Wood and
representing in its full bloom of life and
development, the ultimate Yang. Season-
ally it corresponds to the summer, to peak
growth and fulfilment just prior to the
maturity and consolidation of the Earth
Element (which compares to a late Indian
summer).

This element is full of life, an adolescent
period, savouring the joy of growth and the
energy of activity. It is packed with potential for what could be, but its expansive
character is restrained by Water, that has
the ability to extinguish its flame. In its
turn Fire controls Metal, modifying its
solid structure.

The characteristics of the element and
the signs of balance and imbalance can be
used as indications of direction towards the
appropriate meridians for treatment and
also as tools to help you understand your
horse on a daily basis.

## Characteristics of the Fire Element

| | |
|---|---|
| Season: | Summer |
| Time of day: | Noon |
| Energy quality: | Expanding |
| Colour: | Red/purple |
| Smell: | Burnt |
| Taste: | Bitter |
| Sense: | Speech |
| High tide time: | 11am – 3pm<br>(Heart 11am – 1pm/Small Intestine 1pm – 3pm)<br><br>7pm – 11pm<br>(Heart Protector 7pm – 9pm/<br>Triple Heater 9pm – 11pm) |
| Emotion: | Joy |
| Voice tone: | Laughter/stuttering |
| Tissue: | Blood vessels |
| Concepts: | Protection and circulation |

## Signs of balance/imbalance

### Signs of balance:

- Confident
- Self-assured
- Communicative
- Protective of others

### Signs of imbalance:

- Self-protective nature
- Hypersensitive
- Nervous
- Poor circulation
- Agitation

## Recognising the Fire horse

### Appearance

- Happy in the show or dressage arena, this horse has a natural grace and flowing stride that are a joy to watch.

### Character

- A sensitive rider will find that this horse is highly intuitive to the feelings of his rider.
- His happy, joyful and vibrant personality makes him fun to own.
- This horse will benefit from work that makes the most of his own natural style and capitalises on his love of showing off.
- This is an easy horse to build up an empathetic relationship with as he has such an easy-going, fun-loving character and a rider with the same qualities will get the best out of him.
- Work and fuss need to be evenly balanced with the Fire horse. He loves to be fussed and groomed.
- A relationship with this horse is a very satisfying one as he is totally trusting of those that care for him and bonds well.
- This horse is no bother in the field or with other horses as he extends his sociable nature to equines as well as humans.

### Training

- The Fire horse enjoys himself so much in his work, he may be inclined to anticipate what is required of him or do what

*The Fire horse has a natural grace and flowing stride that are a joy to watch.*

he thinks his rider is going to want. Work carefully on his attention to your aids.

- Do not be slow to praise or reward this horse, he thrives on pleasing his rider.
- This horse is athletic and finds changes of stride and direction easy.
- Speed or endurance do not come easily to this horse.
- Don't push this horse too hard but work with his relaxed and laid-back approach to life and you will achieve the best results.
- Keep a varied work programme to satisfy the curiosity of this horse. He relishes learning new things and if bored may find focussing on the task at hand a problem.
- If this horse is not adequately occupied he may compensate with hyperactivity.

Health
- Present plenty of opportunities for this horse to drink as he will become dehydrated very easily.
- This horse will benefit from regular turnout and activity as he may be prone to circulatory problems.
- A bad circulation may result in this horse feeling the cold – keep an eye on this.
- This is an easy-going, trusting horse that expects the same from its rider. He will be sensitive to any antagonistic emotions.
- This horse enjoys life in his own little world and may be surprised by outside influences. Be prepared for spookiness.
- If this horse becomes bored or spends too much time in his stable he may show signs of stress and boredom such as tongue lolling, lip flapping or weaving.

### Horse/rider relationship

A well-balanced Fire rider will get on well with a Fire horse being able to read his subtle body signals through her seat. The Fire rider will know through experience that touch is important to the Fire horse and will use this to help keep stress levels at a minimum. The Earth rider also works well with the Fire horse being able to help ground and calm any of the Fire horse's over sensitivity and hysteria. The Fire horse does not work so well with Metal, Wood and Water riders.

# The Fire Meridians

## The Small Intestine Meridian

The Small Intestine Meridian begins on the outside of the foreleg, just above the coronet band, one third of the distance between the centre front and centre back of the hoof. It then travels up the leg to the elbow where it follows the top line of the humerus and then turns to cross the top of the scapula bone. It progresses up the neck, towards the head across the jawbone and finishes on the outside of the base of the ear.

*The Small Intestine and Heart Meridians are controlled by the Fire Element.*

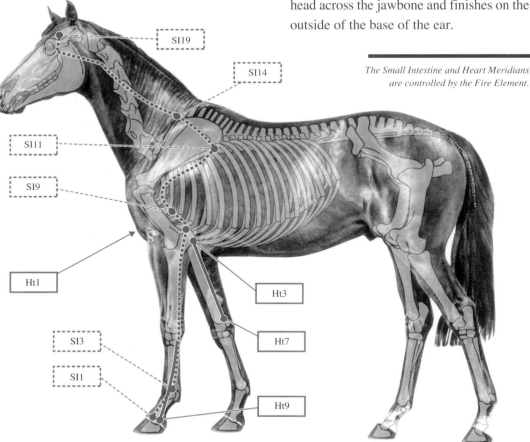

SI19
SI14
SI11
SI9
Ht1
Ht3
Ht7
SI3
SI1
Ht9

.............. *Small Intestine Meridian*
————— *Heart Meridian*

## Small Intestine 1 (SI1)

This is located just above the coronet band, one third of the distance from the centre front to the centre back of the hoof. Indications: Laminitis, pedal osteitis, poor milk production, fever.

## Small Intestine 3 (SI3)

Also known as Quian Chan Wan (thoracic fetlock)
This is just above the fetlock joint in a depression on the outer lower edge of the cannon bone, below the splint bone. Indications: arthritis of the fetlock, knee pain, secondary point for laminitis. Calms the mind.

## Small Intestine 9 (SI9)

Also known as Jian Zhen (steadfast shoulder)
This point is above the humerus in a depression created by the long and lateral heads of the triceps brachi. Indications: shoulder pain, twisted shoulder, strained elbow, paralysis of ulnar or radial nerve. Reflex point.

## Small Intestine 11 (SI11)

Also known as Fei Pan (lung hugging)
This is on the back border of the scapula cartilage. It is on the deltoid and triceps brachi muscles, towards the tail. Indications: pain in the forelimb, arthritis of the shoulder joint, cough, pneumonia.

## Small Intestine 14 (SI14)

Also known as Bo Jian (shoulder tip)
This is in a depression in front of the scapula at the angle of the shoulder blade nearest the head. Indications: pain in the thoracic limb, arthritis of the shoulder.

## Small Intestine 19 (SI19)

Also known as Shan Guan (upper joint)
This is above the temporomandibular joint (TMJ) and below the intertragic notch in a depression just forward of the base of the ear. (This is evident when the mouth is open). Indications: facial paralysis and tension.

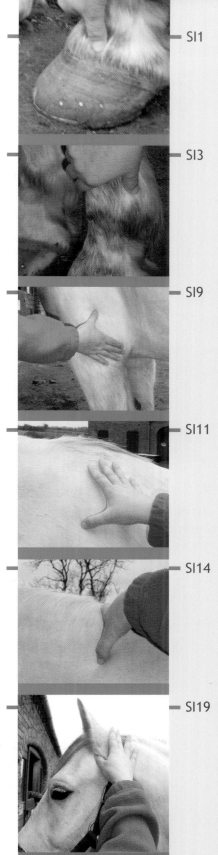

SI1

SI3

SI9

SI11

SI14

SI19

## The Heart Meridian

The heart meridian originates at the heart and emerges on the inside of the shoulder joint. It travels down to the inside back edge of the ulna on the rearwards edge of the carpus.

It then crosses behind the knee to the outside of the leg and descends, ending just above the coronet band, two thirds of the distance between the centre front and centre back of the hoof.

### Heart 1 (Ht1)
Also known as Jia Qu (axilla)
This emerges in the centre of the armpit, on the inside of the axillary artery, between the trunk and the inside leg, over the superficial pectoral muscle.
Indications: sprain of the thoracic limb, shoulder lameness, paralysis of the scapular nerve, pain in the chest and cardiac region.

### Heart 3 (Ht3)
Still on the inside of the leg, this point lies between the back edge of the transverse cubital crease and the inside epicondyle of the humerus.
Indications: arthritis of the elbow. Calms the mind.

### Heart 7 (Ht7)
This point is on the back edge of the radius, just above the accessory carpal bone at the point where the flexor carpi ulnaris inserts into the bone.
Indications: reflex point for the shoulder, fetlock and hoof, arthritis of the carpal joints.

### Heart 9 (Ht9)
Also known as Qian Tui Men (heel of the hoof)
The meridian is now on the outside of the foreleg and ends just above the coronet band, two thirds of the distance from the centre front to the centre back of the hoof.
Indications: inflammation of the heel, laminitis.

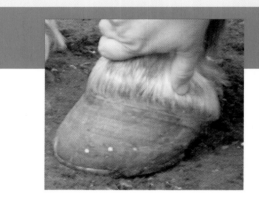

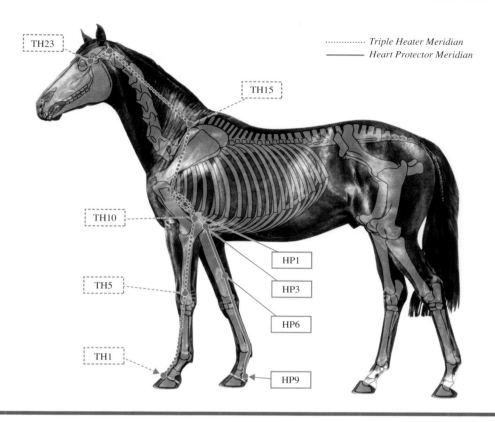

*The Fire Element also controls the Triple Heater and Heart Protector Meridians.*

## The Triple Heater Meridian

This meridian starts at the front of the coronet band of the front foot and runs upwards on the outside of the leg to just above the point of the elbow. From here it follows the upper line of the humerus until it reaches the humeral scapula junction, where it crosses the scapula (shoulder blade), moving upwards to a point just in front of the front border of the shoulder blade. It travels up the side of the neck to the back of the ear and finishes just above the rearmost corner of the eye.

## Triple Heater 1 (TH1)

Also known as Qia Ti Tou (toe of the hoof)
The meridian starts just above the coronet band at midpoint of the front foot.
Indications: laminitis, sidebone, pain in the leg, conjunctivitis, throat problems, colic, fever, convulsions.

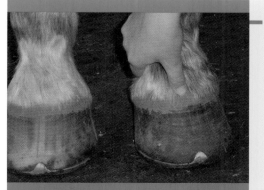

TH1

TH5

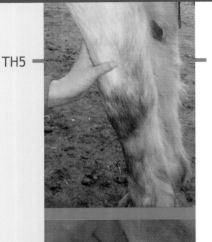

## Triple Heater 5 (TH5)

**Also known as Guo Liang(passing beam)**

**Regulates Yang**

This is found in a depression at the lower end of the radius between the lateral digital extensor and the common digital extensor.

Indication: contraction of tendons, analgesia point, pain in the neck, elbow and shoulder.

TH10

## Triple Heater 10 (TH10)

**Also known as Zhou Shu (elbow association point)**

This is in a depression at the elbow where the humerus joins the radius, over the lateral head of the triceps.

Indications: pain in the shoulder and forelimb; general weakness, wobbler syndrome.

TH15

## Triple Heater 15 (TH15)

**Also known as Fei Men (lung gate)**

This is on the part of the shoulder blade closest to the head in a depression where the bone joins the scapula cartilage.

Indications: shoulder pain.

TH23

## Triple Heater 23 (TH23)

**Also known as Zhuan Nao (turning brain)**

This meridian finishes just above the rearmost corner of the eye on the lower zygomatic process of the frontal bone.

Indications: fever and epilepsy.

## The Heart Protector Meridian

The Heart Protector Meridian starts in the pericardium of the heart and emerges between the fifth rib and the inside of the elbow. It then runs down the back of the inside of the leg until it reaches the Ting point (HP9) between the bulbs of the heel.

### Heart Protector 1 (HP1)
**Also known as Cheng Deng (stirrup)**
This point is between the fifth and sixth rib and the inside of the elbow. It is located on the body rather than on the leg.
Indications: pain in the chest, foot problems. Diagnosis point for foot problems such as navicular disease, pedal osteitis and abscesses.

### Heart Protector 3 (HP3)
This is on the inside of the cubital crease of the elbow to the inside of the biceps muscle. This is also located on the body rather than the leg.
Indications: fever

### Heart Protector 6 (HP6)
**Also known as Ye Yan (chestnut)**
This is on the inside of the front leg, just forward of the chestnut.
Indications: important point for the heart, throat, chest and shoulders, gastritis. Regulates the heart, Chi and blood, calms the mind, harmonises the stomach.

### Heart Protector 9 (HP9)
This is found in the central depression between the bulbs of the heel.
Indications: hoof problems, forelimb pain, arthritis of the fetlock and carpal joint, tendinitis, fever, anxiety, lack of sexual interest.

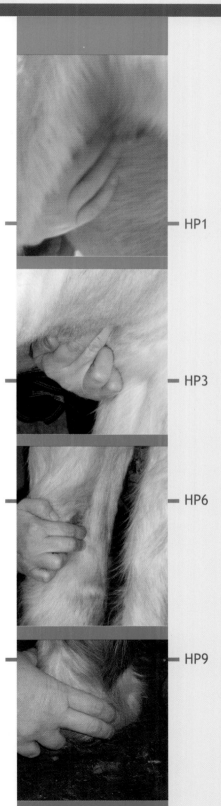

HP1

HP3

HP6

HP9

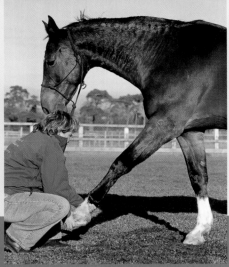

Small intestine 1.                                          2.    3.

## Stretches for the Fire Element

### Small Intestine

1. Stand at a 45 degree angle to the front legs of the horse, facing the tail, and pick the front leg up, resting your outside elbow on your outside knee. Moving from your ankles, gently circle the leg left, right and in a figure of eight.

2. Gently step backwards taking the leg straight forward.
3. If you have help, stretch the head and neck to the opposite side, if not, do this after your leg stretch.
4. Now gently adduct the leg and try pointing the toe.

### Heart

1. Stand at a 45 degree angle to the front legs, facing the tail, and pick the front leg up,

Heart 1.    2.

4.

Triple heater 1.

2.

3.

resting your outside elbow on your out-side knee. Gently circle the leg left, right and in a figure of eight.

2. Gently step backwards, taking the leg forward and abduct. Stretch the bulbs of heels away. Try pointing the toe.

## Triple Heater

1. Stand at a 45 degree angle to the front legs of the horse, facing the tail, and pick the front leg up, resting your outside elbow on your outside knee. Moving from your ankles, gently circle the leg left, right and in a figure of eight.

2. Bring the horse's head down and flex gently to the opposite side to that which you are working. Use side to side movements to bring the head down (use a carrot if necessary).

3. Now pick up the leg once again and gently step backwards taking the leg with you and adduct – if possible hold TH5 with your finger. Whilst in this stretched position, stroke your hand down the outside of the leg from the top and off at the hoof.

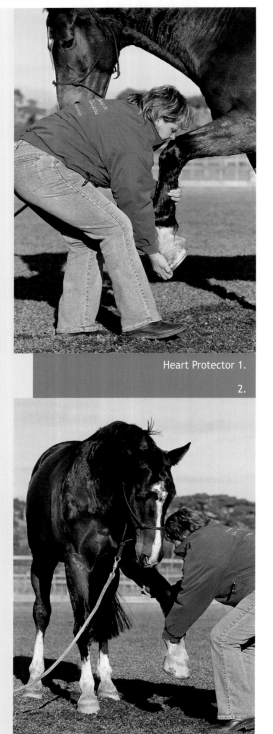

Heart Protector 1.

2.

## Heart Protector

1. Stand at a 45 degree angle to the front legs, facing the tail and pick the front leg up, resting your outside elbow on your outside knee. Moving from your ankles, gently circle the leg left, right and in a figure of eight.
2. Gently step backwards taking the leg straight forward and flex the toe. Then, supporting the back of the knee, gently but firmly stroke the leg downwards. Abducting the leg away from the body. The horse should not be tied up tightly, as he will need to balance.

# The small intestine

The small intestine begins at the pyloric muscle at the exit of the stomach. Its coils lie within the stomach and are attached to the stomach roof by a double layer of peritoneal membrane known as mesentry. The mesentery also carries blood vessels and nerves for the gut. The small intestine can move relatively freely except for the points at which it is attached to the stomach and the caecum.

In the small intestine food eaten by the horse is broken down by enzymes from the pancreas and the liver into its basic constituents of proteins, fats and carbohydrates, which are then absorbed into the blood

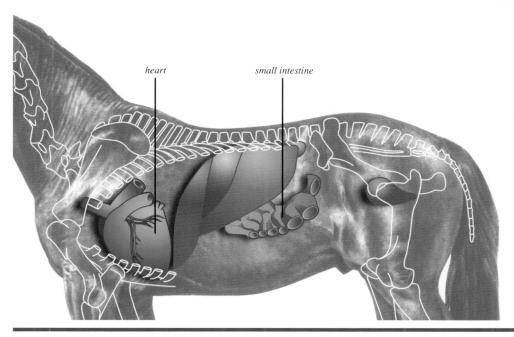

*Position of the small intestine and the heart within the horse's body.*

stream and used for energy and growth. It is between 20 – 27m (65 – 88ft) in length with a diameter that has been described as being greater than a garden hose but smaller than a fireman's canvas hose and has three different areas along its length all with different digestive responsibilities:

• Duodenum first 3 ft (0.9m) approx.
• Jejunum 65ft (20m) long approx.
• Ileum 3 – 5ft (2m) long approx.

These three together can hold up to 50 litres (12 gallons) of material. Food is transported through the small intestine by means of peristalsis or muscular contractions that also help mix it with the digestive juices and push the food against the intestinal wall to aid absorption. The intestinal wall has little 'fingers' along it called villi.

The horse has no gall bladder and is a trickle feeder. Bile trickles continuously into the duodenum from the liver via the bile duct. Feeding little and often is therefore essential for good digestion and efficient use of food.

*The villi help aid absorption of nutrients into the horse's system by increasing the surface area.*

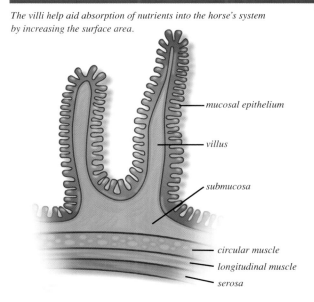

## The duodenum

This is the upper part of the small intestine and it is here that the breaking down process begins. It forms an S-shaped bend that contains the pancreas. The pancreatic and bile ducts enter the duodenum approximately 150mm (6") from the pyloric sphincter muscle of the stomach. The duodenum contains alkaline pancreatic juice – sodium bicarbonate – which counters the acidity of the stomach. The duodenum also contains the following enzymes:

| | |
|---|---|
| **Trysin** | breaks down proteins into peptides then amino acids |
| **Amylase** | breaks down the starch into maltose |
| **Maltae** | breaks down the maltose into glucose |

## Jejunum and ileum

Both the jejunum and ileum lie to the left side of the abdomen between the stomach and the pelvis. The average diameter of the jejunum and ileum is approximately 6 – 7 cm. Whilst there is no exact division between the jejunum and ileum, the last metre is slightly thicker, which defines the ileum, and there is a valve to control flow into the caecum from the small intestines.

At this stage in the digestive process of most animals the food is a creamy smooth mixture. In the horse however it still has coarse fibre in it that is partially broken down in the hindgut by the many thousands of friendly bacteria. From the jejunum amino acids, glucose, minerals and vitamins all pass into the blood stream and some fatty acids and glyceral pass into the lymphatic system.

### Small intestine disorders include:

Strangulation

Impaction

Malabsorption

# The heart

The heart of an average 16hh horse weighs approximately 9lb (4kg). As the horse gets fitter it can increase to 12lb (5.5kg). Although this may at first seem huge, the heart of a horse is proportionally smaller to his body mass than that of other mammals and relies on the pumping action of the hooves and muscles to help pump the venous blood back up the legs to the heart and lungs.

The heart is found in the middle of the chest, nestling into the lungs. Surrounding the heart is a smooth membrane called the pericardium that forms a protective, fluid filled sack around the heart.

The heart is the pump that primarily moves the blood around the body. It consists of four chambers divided by walls of cardiac muscle that do not fatigue. The circulatory system transports oxygen, nutrients and other materials to the cells and transports waste products back to the various eliminatory organs.

## As a rule:
- Vessels carrying blood away from the heart are called arteries
- Vessels carrying blood to the heart are called veins

## Therefore:
- The pulmonary artery carries deoxygenated blood from the heart to the lungs
- The pulmonary vein carries oxygenated blood from the lungs back to the heart

## The four chambers of the heart
As we have said, the heart consists of four chambers, divided into a left and a right side. The right-hand side of the heart is separate from the left-hand side and there is not normally any interaction between the two.

On each side blood enters the top chamber (atrium) through a vessel, passes into the second chamber and leaves the bottom chamber (ventricle) via another large vessel. On both sides, the top chamber merely pumps the blood through to the bottom chamber.

The right atrium (or auricle) receives deoxygenated blood from the veins, via the superior vena cava (vein). When the atrium is

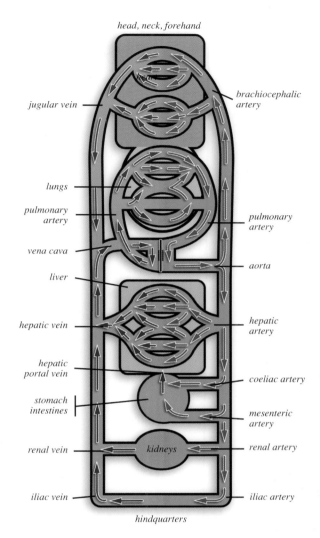

*The circulatory system*

*This diagram shows the progress of blood through the horse's system. The blue blood is deoxygenated and the red, oxygenated.*

full, the blood is passed through the tricuspid valve to the right ventricle. The tricuspid valve closes to prevent any backflow of blood creating the lub of the lub dub of the horse's heartbeat.

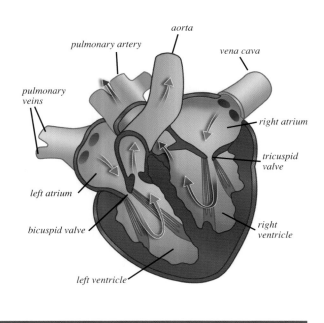

*aorta*

*pulmonary artery*

*vena cava*

*pulmonary veins*

*right atrium*

*tricuspid valve*

*left atrium*

*right ventricle*

*bicuspid valve*

*left ventricle*

*The weight of an average 16hh horse's heart can be anywhere between 9-12lbs.*

The right ventricle then contracts, pushing blood into the pulmonary artery (see above) and on to the lungs. Once in the lungs the blood comes into close contact with the alveoli and a gaseous exchange takes place, whereby carbon dioxide is exchanged for oxygen.

The oxygenated blood now returns to the heart by pulmonary vein to the left atrium. Once full, the blood is pushed under pressure into the left ventricle through the bicuspid valve that close to prevent back flow. The left ventricle has the thickest muscular walls as it has the powerful task of sending oxygenated blood through to the rest of the body (with the exception of the lungs) at great pressure via the aorta (the largest artery in the body).

Semi lunar valves at the exit to the aorta and pulmonary valves at the exit to the pulmonary artery prevent back flow into the left and right ventricles. These create the dup of the lup dup of the heartbeat.

Both sides of the heart work in parallel. The atria fill together and the ventricles contract together.

The heart, unlike any other muscle in the body, does not work by use of the voluntary or involuntary nervous system. It is, in fact, a self-contained unit with its own nervous system call SAN (sino atrial node). This works rather like a pacemaker.

The resting heart of the horse beats 28 – 45 times per minute but can go as high as 200 beats when exerted. If the heartbeat raises and stays raised, this is a sign of distress and pain.

The action of the heart muscle relaxing before and during the process of filling is known as diastolic action. The contraction of the heart muscle as it empties is known as systolic action.

## Main arteries and their responsibilities

Each of the main arteries that feed the organs of the body have specific definable names. These are:

Brachiocephalic artery
  supplies the head and forelegs

Celiac artery
supplies the stomach, liver and spleen
Mesenteric arteries
supply the intestines
Renal artery
supplies the kidneys
Iliac arteries
supply the hindquarters
Femoral artery
supplies the thigh region

The exception to this rule is that the blood from the intestines needs to be filtered by the liver before going into general circulation. This blood is collected into the hepatic portal vein that divides within the liver into a capillary network for filtration purposes before regrouping to form the hepatic vein that goes into the vena cava.

## Direct disorders of the circulatory system include:

- Anaemia
- Shock – potentially life threatening
- Haemorrhage
- Burns and traumatic injury
- Colic
- Heart murmurs – (the sound of a heart valve working imperfectly) can be indicative of arrhythmia or thrombosis
- Arrhythmia - an irregularity of the filling and emptying of the chambers

# The triple heater

In the west we would not consider the triple heater to be an organ. However, it is contained in eastern organ lists, but is seen not to have a shape. It is believed to have a purpose rather than visual or physical dimensions. Its job is to work with the lungs, spleen, bladder, small intestine and kidney, but outside of these duties, it is not seen to exist. Think of it as an organ of energy!

The triple heater (also known as the three burners) helps control heat within the body and is said to guard all the organs of the body – without it they would not work. As the name suggests it is divided into three areas:

- the upper burner encompasses and looks after the warmth in the heart and lungs
- the middle burner encompasses and looks after the warmth in the stomach, spleen, gall bladder, liver and small intestines
- the lower burner encompasses and looks after the large intestines, bladder and kidneys

For optimum health the three burners must work together. If one is not working efficiently and warming the oxygen systems within the area that it looks after, the health and warmth of the mind, body and spirit will be disturbed and continual hot and cold emotions will be experienced, as well as physical upset.

The triple heater corresponds to all the major organs and their corresponding meridians. It would therefore be prudent when treating other meridians to also look at the triple heater to see how strong and clear its energy is.

## The heart protector
(or pericardium)

This does have substance and although not really an organ itself, does the job of protecting the heart. In eastern medicine, classed as an organ, it is in charge of blood and sexual secretions, as well as protecting the heart from all the bumps and bruises of life. In this way it allows the heart to do its job of pumping blood around the body. It is of vital importance for the correct function of the whole. It is this meridian you may use to get into the Heart Meridian, which may not let you in initially as it is too emotionally painful.

## The muscular system

There are three types of muscle tissue, common to all animals:

Cardiac
- striated in appearance and involuntary we have no control over them.

Smooth
- non striated in appearance and involuntary.

Skeletal
- striated in appearance and voluntary we have control over them.

The muscle functions

- Motion.
- Movement of substances within the body. (Cardiac muscles regulate the heart and in this way move blood around the body. Smooth muscle contractions work with the organs, moving food and waste through the gastrointestinal tract (peristalsis), and urine through the urinary system, for example. Whilst the primary function of skeletal muscle contractions is movement, they also help transport blood and lymph.)
- Stabilisation of body position and regulation of organ volume.
- Heat production. As skeletal muscle contracts to perform work, heat is produced. The body uses this to maintain normal body temperature (for example, to warm a cold horse it helps to move it around).

The most relevant muscle group for the Shiatsu practitioner would be the skeletal group.

Skeletal Muscles

Skeletal muscles usually function in groups. Motion is created by the contraction and relaxation of opposing groups and the effect this has on the skeleton. Almost every moveable bone can be activated by more than one muscle and most body movements require simultaneous contraction and relax-

The muscles of a horse: showing key muscles of relevance for a Shiatsu treatment.

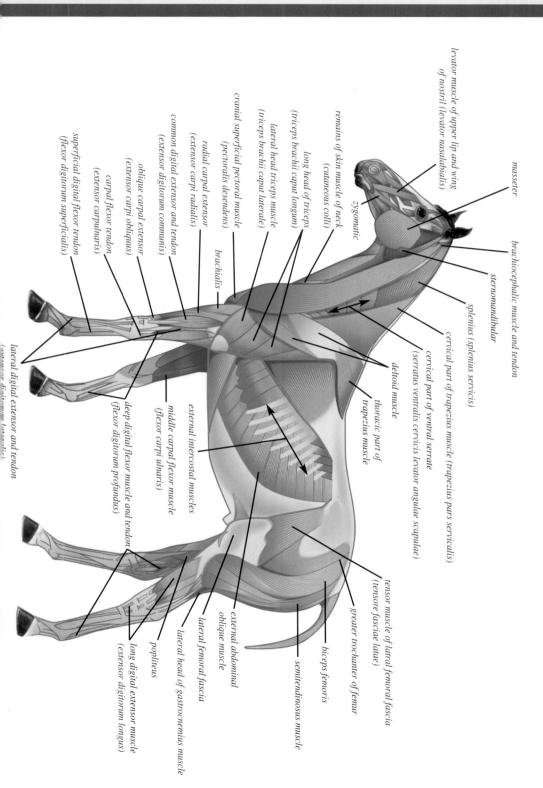

masseter

brachiocephalic muscle and tendon

sternomandibular

splenius (splenius servicis)

cervical part of trapezius muscle (trapezius pars servicalis)

cervical part of ventral serrate (serratus ventralis cervicis levator angulae scapulae)

deltoid muscle

thoracic part of trapezius muscle

tensor muscle of latral femoral fascia (tensore fasciae latae)

greater trochanter of femur

biceps femoris

semitendinosius muscle

external abdominal oblique muscle

lateral femoral fascia

popliteus

long digital extensor muscle (extensor digitorum longus)

lateral head of gastrocnemius muscle

external intercostal muscles

middle carpal (flexor muscle (flexor carpi ularis)

deep digital flexor muscle and tendon (flexor digitorum profundus)

oblique carpal extensor (extensor carpi obliquus)

lateral digital extensor and tendon (extensor digitorum lateralis)

superficial digital flexor tendon (flexor digitorum superficialis)

carpal flexor tendon (extensor carpualnaris)

common digital extensor and tendon (extensor digitorum communis)

radial carpal extensor (extensor carpi radialis)

brachialis

long head of triceps (triceps brachii caput longum)

lateral head triceps muscle (triceps brachii caput laterale)

cranial superficial pectoral muscle (pectoralis desendens)

remains of skin muscle of neck (cutaneous colli)

zygomatic

levator muscle of upper lip and wing of nostril (levator nasolabialis)

ation of several groups of muscles. These break down into three different types with differing functions:

### Prime movers:
Skeletal muscles whose **contractions** are of major importance in producing a particular movement.
### Antagonists:
These produce movement of the same body part as the prime movers, but in the opposite direction, so **lengthening** of the antagonist will stabilise, focus and control the movement produced by the prime mover eg the triceps.
### Synergists:
These steady the body part being moved or stabilise the prime mover, making the action more efficient.

It must be remembered that in order for a muscle to work it must contract – muscles do not pull.

In an animal that relies on speed, the muscle is pale. However if the animal relies on dexterity and stamina the muscle appears redder. This difference in colour has three causes:

### Redder muscles have
- a greater quantity of energy-producing pigments, especially myoglobin
- enhanced blood circulation
- a greater number of mitochondria in the muscle cells, known as slow-twitch muscle fibres, which work aerobically

### Paler muscles have
- a smaller quantity of energy producing pigments
- functional blood circulation
- a composition of fibres that are much less dependent on oxygen, create a denser muscle and store more muscle sugar. These are known as fast-twitch muscle fibres

*Slow twitch* muscle fibres respond to training for increasing fitness in slow to medium work and theoretically can work forever – they do not tire.

*Fast twitch* muscle fibres produce greater quantities of lactic acid and hydrogen ions in the absence of oxygen. This build up results in a shorter working time. The result is that they are suitable for short bursts of action as in galloping.

However there is a third sub-group – *fast twitch high oxidative* – which exists in varying proportions in all horse muscle fibre (from one third to one half). These are important as they can be 'trained' to work aerobically thus increasing the horse's stamina and dexterity.

Any one muscle is made up of slow and fast-twitch fibres but the proportion is what gives the muscle its characteristics. This proportion is determined genetically.

Aerobic fibres are the cornerstone of muscular tone. In a fit horse they are constantly ready to perform their function. Anaerobic fibres generate short, strong bursts of power and are generally used for propulsion.

If a horse is injured or tired the muscles spasm, reducing, and sometimes preventing, action.

A muscle works to its full potential when all fibres are in play; the strength of effect is commensurate with the number of fibres working. When a muscle is toned it can be stretched to its full potential by its opposite number. However when tired, over-stretching and subsequent tearing can occur.

These muscle fibres, and bundles of fibres, are covered in connective tissue that joins together to form a tendon attaching the muscle to the bones (and occasionally, to cartilage and skin). Usually muscles and their tendons cross one joint, producing movement at that joint and usually greater movement in one bone.

The point of attachment of a muscle nearest the trunk is called its origin. The point of attachment of the muscle that produces the greatest movement when the muscle contracts is called the insertion.

In horses, the key propulsive muscles are in the quarters, the thigh, the shoulder and the neck.

## Muscles of the trunk (appertaining to the Fire Element)

Individual muscles are the practitioner's primary source of location of points on the meridians and it is important to know where they originate from and go to, as well as their function.

### Trapezius – thoracic

| | |
|---|---|
| Origin | nuchal and supraspinous ligaments from C2 – T10 |
| Insertion | dorsal third of scapular spine |
| Functions | elevates shoulder, draws scapula cranio dorsally and caudo dorsally |

### Latissimus dorsi

| | |
|---|---|
| Origin | supraspinous ligament from T3 caudally via thoracolumbar fascia |
| Insertion | teres major tuberosity of humerus with teres major muscle |
| Functions | retracts limb, flexes shoulder joint, when limb is fixed, draws trunk cranially |

### Serratus ventralis (cervical/dorsal)

| | |
|---|---|
| Origin | transverse process of C4-C7/first 8 or 9 ribs |
| Insertion | scapular cartilage and two adjacent triangular areas on medial surface of scapula |
| Functions | suspends trunk; raises neck when forelimb is fixed, may support inspiration |

## Deep pectorals

| | |
|---|---|
| Origin | sternum, distally on ribs 4-9; tunica flava abdominus |
| Insertion | major and minor tubercles of humerus; tendon of origin of coracobrachialis |
| Functions | suspends trunk between forelimbs; retracts limb, stabilises shoulder joint |

## Rectus abdominis

| | |
|---|---|
| Origin | lateral surface of costal cartilages 4 – 9 |
| Insertion | pre-pubic tendon and via accessory ligament on head of femur |
| Functions | compresses abdominal viscera, flexes the trunk, flexes lumbar spine and lumbo-sacral joint |

## External abdominal obliques

| | |
|---|---|
| Origin | lateral surface of ribs 4-18; thoracolumbar fascia |
| Insertion | abdominal tendon, linea alba and prepubic tendon, pelvic tendon, coxal tuber, inguinal ligament |
| Functions | compresses abdominal viscera, flexes the trunk |

## Tensor fascia latae

| | |
|---|---|
| Origin | coxal tuber (of illium – point of haunch) |
| Insertion | patella, lateral border of patellar ligament, cranial border of tibia with superficial gluteal muscle on third trochanter |
| Functions | Flexes hip joint, protracts hind limb, and extends stifle |

## Biceps femoris

| | |
|---|---|
| Origin | vertebral head spinous and transverse processes of last three sacral vertebrae, sacrosciatic ligament and tail fascia, pelvic head – ischial tuberosity (point of buttock) |
| Insertion | patella, lateral and medial patellar ligament; cranial border of tibia, crural fascia |
| Functions | extends hip and stifle; caudal part flexes stifle, abducts hind limb and extends hock |

## Superficial gluteal muscle

| | |
|---|---|
| Origin | coxal tuber |
| Insertion | 3rd trochanter and fascia latae |
| Functions | flexes hip joint, protracts and abducts hind limb |

*Key*
*C = cervical vertebrae*    *L = lumbar vertebrae*
*T = thoracic vertebrae*    *S = sacral vertebrae*

*Adapted from Anatomy of the Horse by*
*Klaus Dieter Budras, W G Sack and Sabine Rock.*

# The Earth Element

•

## Governing the Stomach and Spleen Meridians

In the creative cycle it would be easy to misunderstand the Earth Element as a sad element. Following on from the exuberant growth of Fire, it is the beginning of energy transforming onto a downward path towards the stillness of winter. This misunderstanding would be a mistake. This is a well-balanced, knowledgeable element. Think of the glorious days of an Indian summer when you are aware of the harder times to come and have the experience to savour the moment. Or the end of a season when all the qualities of that time seem to gather together in a glorious celebration – this is Earth.

This is where ideas are generated, opinions formed and compassion and understanding expressed. As the fiery reds of the Fire Element settle down and cool into the yellows and oranges that represent Earth, maturity follows. In its turn Earth condenses into Metal. In the controlling Ko cycle, Earth limits the flow of water whilst its own gravitas is supported and held by Wood.

The characteristics of the element and the signs of balance and imbalance can be used as indications of direction towards the appropriate meridians for treatment and also as tools to help you understand your horse on a daily basis.

## Characteristics of the Earth Element

| | |
|---|---|
| Season | Late summer/early autumn |
| Time of day | Afternoon |
| Energy quality | Downwards and descending |
| Colour | Brown/orange |
| Smell | Rotten (sweet) |
| Taste | Sweet |
| Sense | Taste |
| High Tide Time | 7am – 11am<br>(stomach 7am-9am/spleen 9am – 11am) |
| Emotion | Compassion |
| Voice tone | Singsong, lilting |
| Tissue | Flesh |
| Concepts | Nourishment / fertility / support / stability / grounding |

## Signs of balance/imbalance

### Signs of balance
- flesh well toned
- easy going/easy to be with
- patient, stable, steady personality
- loves and needs routine

### Signs of imbalance
- unusual shape ie very thin/heavy belly/saggy flesh
- looks sick (eg cheeks hang)
- pushy/stubborn
- communicates by not communicating
- puffy limbs – particularly hind limbs
- lack of confidence, shy
- heavy, purposeful walk

*The Earth horse is an amiable horse
and has a very kind nature.*

## Recognising the Earth horse

- This is a solid horse deep set through the girth.
- A strong body with healthy muscle tone makes him a hardy character.
- A good doer, he may be prone to putting on weight.

### Characteristics

- The Earth horse is the perfect horse for nervous riders as he has an amiable, reliable personality.
- This horse will be inclined to look after his rider.
- In both riding and handling this horse a rider is unlikely to experience any difficulties as he has a very kind nature.
- This is great horse to learn how to handle equines on as he has a huge store of patience.
- There are very few situations that will flap or unsettle the Earth horse.
- As long as he is well looked after the Earth horse tends to be satisfied with his lot and well grounded.

### Health

- A good doer, this horse may be prone to laminitis and is likely to be sensitive to any form of sugar. His keeper should look at feeds low in molasses and feed plenty of roughage.
- Food is quite important to this horse and he may appear to be very single minded as an expression of greed.
- This horse is sensitive to arthritis and rheumatism. Avoid any damp situations.

### Training

- Harness this horse's energy levels and whilst he is not nimble or fast, he can be trained to an adequate standard in most disciplines.

- This horse needs a regular, consistent work programme, focused on muscular activity, to keep him fit and active.

### Horse/rider relationship

The patience and tolerance exhibited by the Earth horse makes him an ideal riding school, novice or children's mount. He will look after his rider, maintaining a sense of balance and harmony. For this reason he would be the perfect mount for the Water rider, where timidity or fear is uppermost. However, his tendency to fatigue easily when out of balance would also work well with a sen-

sitive Fire rider whose own enthusiasm for activity, tempered with intuitive feelings for her mount, could help promote energy.

## The Earth Meridians

### The Stomach Meridian

The stomach meridian begins on the lower eyelid, just forward of the centre of the eyelid. From here it travels nosewards to a point

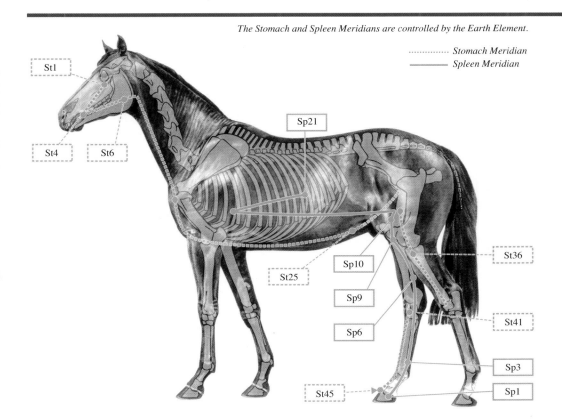

*The Stomach and Spleen Meridians are controlled by the Earth Element.*

............... *Stomach Meridian*
————— *Spleen Meridian*

St1

Sp21

St4    St6

St36

Sp10

St25

Sp9

St41

Sp6

Sp3

St45    Sp1

on the cheek just before the corner of the mouth. It then runs towards the tail through the middle of the jowl and down the neck in the groove between the sternomandibular muscle and the lower part of the bronchiocephalic muscle until it reaches a point just in front of the point of the shoulder. The meridian continues down in between the front legs and along the belly, 1.5 cun away from the midline ending in the groin. Now running down the outside of the back leg on the front of the tibia, it then switches to the inside of the leg, ending just above the coronet band, at the centre point.

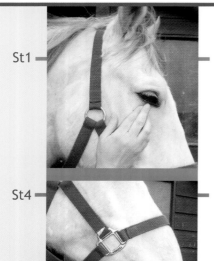

St1

### Stomach 1 (St1)

**Also known as Jing Ming (clear eye)**

This is on the lower eyelid, just forward of the midpoint

Indications: conjunctivitis, keratitis, equine recurrent uveitis, corneal ulcers, facial paralysis.

St4

### Stomach 4 (St4)

**Also known as Suo Kuo (locking mouth)**

0.5 cun from the corner of the mouth, where the levator nasolabialis and zygomaticus muscles meet to create a V-junction

Indications: facial paralysis, hypersalivation, lingual paralysis, maxillary and mandibular disorders, mastication problems, facial swelling, tetanus, tranquilisation.

St6

### Stomach 6 (St6)

When the jaw is open, this is found on the main bulk of the jaw bone in a depression in the centre of the masseter muscle.

Indications: lung disorders, facial paralysis, facial swelling, maxillary and mandibular disorders, mastication problems, tetanus, tranquilisation.

## Stomach 25 (St25)

This lies on the belly 2 cun to the side of the belly button.
Indications: gastrointestinal disorders, diarrhoea.

## Stomach 36 (St36)

**Also known as Hou San Li (pelvic 3 miles)**

This is found on the outside of the leg at the top of the tibia, 1 cun away from its crest over the cranial tibialis muscle.
Indications: motor point of the cranial tibialis muscle, tibial and fibular pain, stifle pain, patellar luxation, arthritis of the tarsal joint, paralysis of the tibial and fibular nerves, gastrointestinal disorders, immunostimulation, fever, anorexia, lethargy. (Pain relieving effects).

## Stomach 41 (St41)

The meridian then swaps to the inside of the leg between the long and lateral digital extensor at a point level with the malleolus, where the tarsus and metatarsus meet.
Indications: pain in the hock, motor impairment, abdominal disorders.

## Stomach 45 (St45)

**Also known as Hou Ti Tou (toe of the hind hoof)**

This lies just above the coronet band in the centre of the toe.
Indications: laminitis, ringbone, sidebone, navicular disease, all hoof problems, convulsions, colic, stifle problems.

St25

St36

St41

St45

The Spleen Meridian

This meridian starts just above the coronet band of the hind leg on the inside of the hoof, one third of the distance from the centre front to the centre back of the hoof. It then runs up the inside of the leg to a point just in front of the lower part of the femur. From here it travels forwards across the lower part of the ribs to a point in the 4th intercostal space. Next it turns back on itself and runs slightly higher ending at a point in the 10th intercostal space at the level of the junction between the shoulder blade and the humerus.

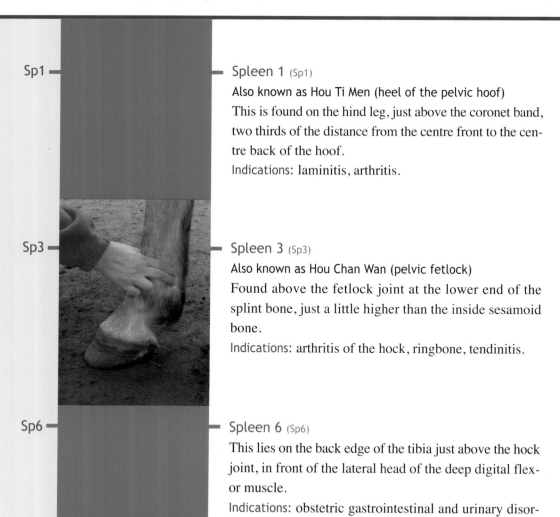

Sp1

Sp3

Sp6

**Spleen 1** (Sp1)
Also known as Hou Ti Men (heel of the pelvic hoof)
This is found on the hind leg, just above the coronet band, two thirds of the distance from the centre front to the centre back of the hoof.
Indications: laminitis, arthritis.

**Spleen 3** (Sp3)
Also known as Hou Chan Wan (pelvic fetlock)
Found above the fetlock joint at the lower end of the splint bone, just a little higher than the inside sesamoid bone.
Indications: arthritis of the hock, ringbone, tendinitis.

**Spleen 6** (Sp6)
This lies on the back edge of the tibia just above the hock joint, in front of the lateral head of the deep digital flexor muscle.
Indications: obstetric gastrointestinal and urinary disorders, immunostimulation.

### Spleen 9 (Sp9)

**Also known as Shen Tan (kidney mansion)**

This can be found on the back edge of the medial condyle of the tibia, over the deep digital flexor muscle and sapheonous vein.

Indications: pain in the pelvis and stifle, diarrhoea, oestrous cycle irregularity, urticaria, poisoning, urinary disorders.

### Spleen 10 (Sp10)

This is on the front edge of the femur, just above the stifle joint, at the back of the bulge created by the quadriceps femoris.

Indications: pain in the stifle, oestrous cycle irregularity, allergy, urticaria, toxaemia.

### Spleen 21 (Sp21)

Found level with the joint of the shoulder blade and humerus in the 10th intercostal space.

Indications: emphysema, laminitis, back pain, liver disorders, general weakness. Useful in finding Bl18 located directly above it.

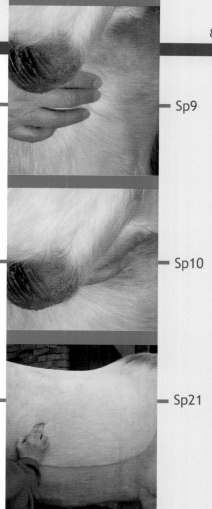

Sp9

Sp10

Sp21

# Stretches for the Earth Element

## Stomach

1. Stand at a 45 degree angle to the back legs of the horse, facing the tail, and pick the back leg up, resting your outside elbow on your outside knee. Moving from your ankles, gently circle the horse's leg left and right and in a figure of eight.

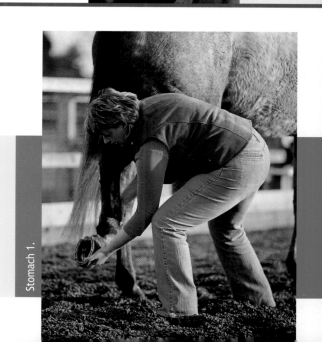

Stomach 1.

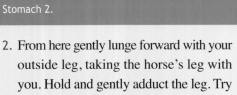

Stomach 2.

3.

2. From here gently lunge forward with your outside leg, taking the horse's leg with you. Hold and gently adduct the leg. Try pointing the toe, listening to the horse at all times.

3. An extra stretch along this meridian would be to raise the head. This could be performed at the same time if you have help. If not do it after the leg stretch.

4.

4. Perform small stretches between your hands along the stomach where the meridian runs.

## Spleen

1. Stand at a 45 degree angle to the back legs of the horse, facing the tail, and pick the back leg up, resting your outside elbow on your outside knee. Moving from your ankles, gently circle the horse's leg left and right and in a figure of eight.

Spleen stretch: 1.  2.  3.

2. Lunge forward with your outside leg, taking the horse's leg with you. Hold and gently abduct the leg. Try flexing the toe, listening to the horse at all times.
3. Again perform small stretches between your hands along the stomach where the Spleen Meridian runs.

## The stomach

The stomach lies within the left half of the abdomen and remains within the protection of the rib cage.

An empty stomach is about the size of a rugby ball. A full stomach can contain 2-5 gallons or 9 – 22 litres of content. No digestion takes place in the horse's mouth but starts once the food reaches the stomach. The mucosal and pyloric glands in its wall excrete gastric juices, which acidify the food by means of hydrochloric acid. This contains three enzymes:

**Pepsin**
which starts breaking down proteins

**Rennin**
which coagulates milk in foals

**Lipase**
which starts to work on lipids in fats and oils

**Plus a small microbial population**

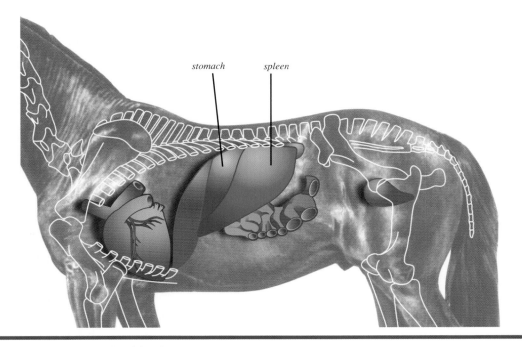

*Position of the stomach and the spleen.*

The horse is a trickle feeder – feeding inappropriately large concentrate feeds can lead to:

• colic
• laboured breathing
• fatigue
• lamintis
• ruptured stomach

A horse takes 24 hours to empty a full stomach but prefers to keep it half full.

Five hours after eating a full meal a horse will usually feel hungry again. The shape of the stomach allows water drunk during or after a feed to pass over the top of the undigested contents rather than washing it out. Therefore there is no need to withhold water during feeds.

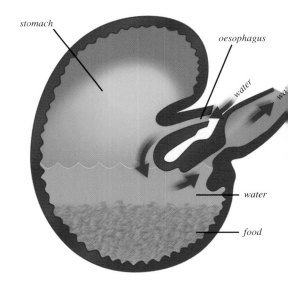

*The shape of the horse's stomach allows water to pass over the top of undigested contents.*

Food leaves the horse's stomach in the following order with the most liquid nutrients leaving first:

- water
- carbohydrate
- proteins
- fat

The ring of muscle controlling the inlet into the stomach is called the cardiac sphincter. The muscle at the outlet are called the pyloric sphincter.

The cardiac sphincter controls the passage of food from the oesophagus into the stomach. This valve is particularly powerful and does not allow food to be regurgitated. The walls of the stomach will burst rather than allow digesta back into the oesophagus, therefore it is important the horse does not consume food that may cause digestive upset. The soft palate hangs like a curtain across the back of the horse's mouth. Should food be rejected from the horse's stomach, this would force it out of the horse's nose rather than the mouth. The presence of food in the nostrils may indicate a ruptured stomach.

## The spleen

The spleen, which is a reservoir for blood cells, is situated near the level of the last rib and on the left side of the abdomen, next to the abdominal wall. It is responsible for cleaning blood cells, for breaking them down when worn out (they are finally deposited in the liver) and for discharging them into the circulation when needed by the horse. A horse can mobilise its blood reserves very quickly, for example when it is exerted.

As a foal matures, the red bone marrow in the long bones is replaced by yellow bone marrow and red cell production is taken over mainly by the spleen.

Superficial muscles of the head, neck and chest (appertaining to the Earth Element)

Individual muscles are the practitioner's primary source of location of points on the meridians and it is important to know where they originate from and go to, as well as their function.

Masseter

| Origin | facial crest/zygomatic arch |
|---|---|
| Insertion | caudolateral on mandible |
| Functions | elevates mandible and presses it against maxilla for mastication |

## Splenius

| | |
|---|---|
| Origin | spinous processes of T3-T5 by means of thoracolumbar fascia/nuchal ligament |
| Insertion | nuchal crest and mastoid process of temporal bone/transverse processes of C2-C5 |
| Functions | extends, elevates or bends neck and head laterally |

## Omotransversarius

| | |
|---|---|
| Origin | shoulder fascia |
| Insertion | transverse processes of C2-C4 |
| Functions | protracts limb, bends neck laterally |

## Cleidomastoideur

| | |
|---|---|
| Origin | clavicular intersection at cranial end of cleidobrachialis |
| Insertion | mastoid process of temporal bone |
| Functions | protracts forelimb, flexes and turns head |

## Sternocephalicus

| | |
|---|---|
| Origin | manubrium sterni |
| Insertion | caudal border of mandible |
| Functions | opens mouth, flexes or inclines head and neck to side of muscle |

## Cutaneous colli

| | |
|---|---|
| Origin | manubrium sterni |
| Insertion | on the superficial fascia covering the jugular groove |
| Functions | tightens and moves the skin on the ventral surface of the neck |

## Pectoralis transversus

| | |
|---|---|
| Origin | costal cartilages of first to sixth ribs and adjacent sternum |
| Insertion | forearm fascia |
| Functions | connects forelimb with trunk, adducts, protracts and retracts forelimb |

Key
C = cervical vertebrae    L = lumbar vertebrae    Adapted from Anatomy of the Horse by
T = thoracic vertebrae    S = sacral vertebrae    Klaus Dieter Budras, W G Sack and Sabine Rock.

# The Metal Element

Governing the Lung
and Large Intestine Meridians

Metal is synonymous with consolidation in the creative cycle. Its seasonal parallel would be with autumn, a time of ripeness and appreciation. It is fed by Earth and in turn dissolves in the Water. It is a strong element, positively inward looking with the ability to dissimilate things into their constituent parts and to create the boundaries that define them. It takes the extreme Yang element of Fire to control Metal which in turn controls Wood either by cutting it down or by containing it.

The characteristics of the element and the signs of balance and imbalance can be used as indications of direction towards the appropriate meridians for treatment and also as tools to help you understand your horse on a daily basis.

## Characteristics of the Metal element

| | |
|---|---|
| Season | Autumn |
| Time of day | Early evening |
| Energy quality | Inward and contracting |
| Colour | White/ashen |
| Smell | Fishy/medicated |
| Taste | Pungent |
| Sense | Smell |
| High Tide Time | 3am – 7 am (Lung 3 am – 5am/ Large intestine 5 am – 7 am) |
| Emotion | Grief |
| Voice Tone | Weeping |
| Tissue | Skin and body hair |
| Concepts | Communication, harmony, connection, rhythm |

## Signs of balance/imbalance

### Signs of balance
- Open personality
- Positive minded
- Emotionally stable
- Sociable
- Clear coat
- Strong vibrant vocal expression

### Signs of imbalance
- Lowered neck
- Tendency to isolation
- Easily manipulated
- Lethargic
- Confused/dark quality

*The Metal horse has a business like approach to his work and likes to get on with the job.*

### Recognising the Metal horse

#### Appearance
- This horse is angular, lean and strong and looks 'well' but not showy.

#### Character
- If you're looking for a horse that gets on with the job and doesn't appreciate a great deal of fuss, the Metal horse is for you.
- This horse will have a business-like approach to his work, without being flashy or temperamental.
- He will be predictable and unlikely to show any spontaneous characteristics.
- However he can be relied upon to do the job he is asked to do.
- In return, he will expect to be treated fairly

and will respond to a respectful relationship with his handler.
- If you are looking for affection, this is not the horse for you as the Metal horse is inclined to be rather aloof.
- This is a difficult horse to build up a relationship with as he tends to keep himself to himself.

#### Health
- Keep an eye on his breathing, as this horse is inclined towards dryness in the lungs and respiratory tract. You may find it necessary to soak his hay and be sure he has plenty of water to hand at all times.
- Keep him warm and work him regularly, as this horse can be prone to chills and muscle complaints.

## Training

- He will thrive in an environment founded on routine.
- This horse is hard work to bond with but it will be worthwhile once a mutual respect is established.
- With a generally well formed physique, this horse is suitable for most disciplines.

## Horse/rider relationship

This horse would work well with a Wood rider, whose strong vital energy and athletic nature would enhance the Metal horse's ability to get any ridden task done efficiently. The Earth rider, who generally gets on with most elements, would also work well with the Metal horse, respecting his need for routine and being patient in building an intuitive relationship.

# The Metal Meridians

## The Lung Meridian

The Lung Meridian starts internally and emerges between the ribs, on the inside of the humerus, on the inside of the cephalic vein (Lu1). It then zigzags upwards and then back down to the forward edge of the axillary fold along the biceps tendon and away from the centre of the body down the inside front edge of the radius, to just above the knee. From here it travels backwards over the knee and cannon bone to end just above the coronet band, two thirds of the distance from the centre front to the centre back of the hoof.

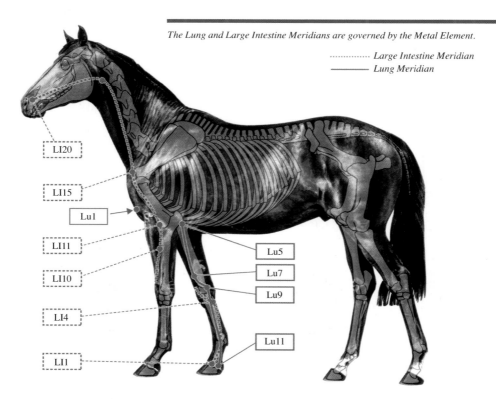

*The Lung and Large Intestine Meridians are governed by the Metal Element.*

················ *Large Intestine Meridian*
————— *Lung Meridian*

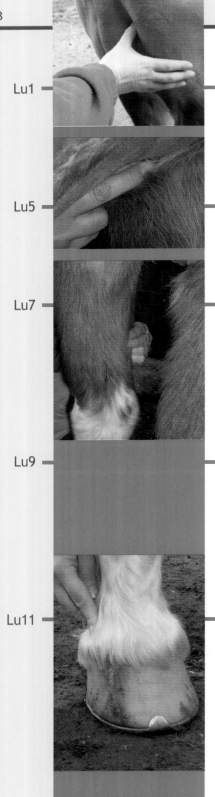

Lu1

Lu5

Lu7

Lu9

Lu11

## Lung 1 (Lu1)

Although internal, Lu1 lies in the first intercostal space directly on the inside of the cephalic vein, next to the humerus.
Indications: cough, pain in the chest, shoulder and back, oedema of the cranial thorax.

## Lung 5 (Lu5)

This is on the inside of the cubital crease on the outside of the tendon of the biceps brachii.
Indications: pain in the elbows, cough.

## Lung 7 (Lu7)

This is found on the inside front edge of the radius, just above the inside styloid process, rearwards of the extensor carpi radialis and forwards of the abductor pollicus longus.
Indications: cough, stiffness and pain in the neck, facial paralysis, tonification of the forelimb. This is a master point for the head and neck.

## Lungs 9 (Lu9)

This is found on the radial side of the knee where the radius and the first row of carpal bones meet, just forward of the accessory carpal bone.
Indications: pain in the chest, asthma, cough, shoulder and back pain, metacarpal arthritis, periostitis, laminitis.

## Lung 11 (Lu11)

**Ting and Wood point**

**Also known as Qian Ti Men (heels of the hoof)**

This is found just above the coronet band, two thirds of the distance from the centre front to the centre back of the hoof.
Indications: immunostimulation, sore throat, respiratory failure, laminitis, pain in the pastern, sidebone, inflammation of the bulbs of the hoof, expistaxis.

## The Large Intestine Meridian

The Large Intestine Meridian begins just above the coronet band on the inside of the leg, one third of the distance from the centre front to the centre back of the hoof. It then moves up the inside of the front of the pastern and crosses in front of the knee to the outside of the leg and continues up to the front of the elbow joint. Here it moves forward in front of the humerus and the shoulder blade joint continuing up the neck, over the larynx and lower jaw bone to a point just before the nostril.

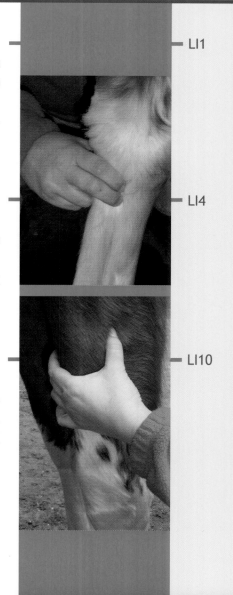

### Large Intestine 1 (LI1)
This is found just above the coronet band on the inside of the foreleg, one third of the distance from the centre front to the centre back of the hoof.
Indications: laminitis, ringbone, sidebone, navicular disease, all hoof problems, fever, pharyngitis.

### Large Intestine 4 (LI4)
Motor point for the dorsal interosseous muscle
This point is on the inside of the foreleg below the knee between the splint bone and the cannon bone.
Indications: pain in the neck, shoulder, forelimb and mouth, immunostimulation, fever.

### Large Intestine 10 (LI10)
Also known as Qian San Li and Thoracic 3 miles
The meridian now wraps around the front of the knee and is found on the outside on the radius in between the extensor carpi radialis and the common digital extensor, 2 cun below LI11.
Indications: pain in the forelimb, radial paralysis, indigestion.

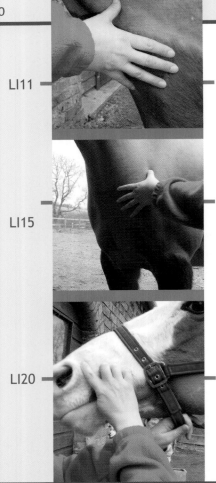

LI11

LI15

LI20

## Large Intestine 11 (LI11)

In a depression forward of the elbow, in the transverse cubital crease, this is easily found when the leg is bent. Indications: arthritis in the elbow, paralysis of the forelimb, fever, pharyngitis, urticaria, abdominal pain, eye pain, immunostimulation.

## Large Intestine 15 (LI15)

**Also known as Jian Jin (shoulder well)**

This is found in a depression forward of the junction of the scapula and humerus in the gap between the two, between the supra spinous and infraspinous muscle. Indications: pain of the forelimb, main point for shoulder pain and arthritis, paralysis of the suprascapular nerve.

## Large Intestine 20 (LI20)

This is found rearwards of the nostrils on the dorsal edge of the caninus muscle.

Indications: cough, cold, sinusitis, rhinitis, congestion of the lungs, urticaria, fever, fatigue, sunstroke.

# Stretches for
# the Metal Element

### Lung

1. Stand at a 45 degree angle to the front legs of the horse, facing the tail and pick up the front leg, resting your outside elbow on your outside knee. Moving from your ankles, circle the leg left and right and in a figure of eight.

2. From here lunge forward towards the tail with your outside leg taking the horse's leg with you. Hold and gently abduct the leg, try pointing the toe, listening to the horse at all times.

## Large Intestine

1. Stand at 45 degrees to the front legs of the horse, facing the tail and pick the front leg up, resting your outside elbow on your outside knee. Moving to your ankle, circle the leg left and right and in a figure of eight.
2. Lunge forward towards the tail with your outside leg taking the horse's leg with you. Hold and gently adduct the leg, pointing the toe – listening to the horse at all times.

3. You can also ask the horse to take his head and neck over to the other side and flex at the poll.

Large Intestine stretch 1.         2.   3.

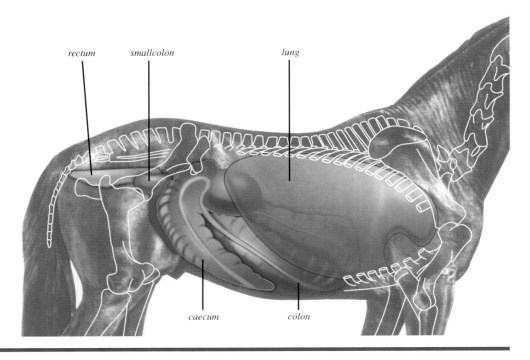

rectum    smallcolon       lung

caecum    colon

*Position of the lungs and the large intestine.*

## The lungs

### The function of the lungs

The lungs are a key component of the respiratory system, providing the necessary environment in which a gaseous exchange, enabling oxygen to be absorbed into the bloodstream and carbon dioxide to be expelled, can take place. All living cells need oxygen to maintain normal body function including breaking glucose down for energy, the metabolism of food and muscle activity.

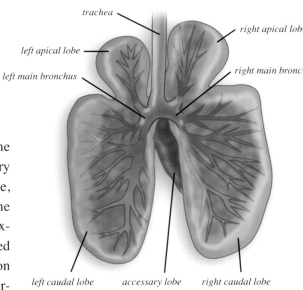

trachea

right apical lob

left apical lobe

right main bronc

left main bronchus

left caudal lobe    accessary lobe    right caudal lobe

*The lungs provide the perfect environment for the exchange of gases – oxygen and carbon dioxide - to take place.*

External respiration involves the exchange of gases between the respiratory organs and the bloodstream. Internal respiration involves the exchange of gases between the bloodstream and the body cells.

## Where the lungs lie

The lungs fit tightly into the chest (thoracic) cavity, the second largest of the body cavities with several other essential organs, the most important of which is the heart. Each lung differs in size and shape. The right lung has an accessory lobe at its base and is larger than the left lung – mainly in width. Lung tissue is soft, spongy and highly elastic. When lungs are collapsed they shrink to a third of their original size. The left lung has a cardiac notch between the third and sixth rib that allows space for the heart. The shape of the chest is maintained by the rib cage that protects the lungs.

## How the horse breathes

When the rib cage expands the diaphragm muscle contracts and the lungs expand to fill the space, creating a vacuum and pulling air in through the nostrils. (The horse cannot breathe through his mouth.)

This air passes through the nasal cavities, where it is brought to body temperature by passing over the turbinate bones that are covered in mucous membranes, and has dust

particles filtered from it by tiny 'hairs', which project from the membranes in the lower airway and are called cilia. This air then passes into the pharynx that contains the soft palate and the epiglottis. The epiglottis acts like a valve directing food into the oesophagus and air into the larynx as appropriate. Only gases may pass through the larynx.

The air then passes through the windpipe or trachea that connects the larynx to the lungs. Just before the lungs, the trachea splits into two bronchi. These branch out, one into each of the lungs and thereafter continue to divide into bronchioles, spreading throughout the lung.

These branches are narrow tubes lined with mucous membrane and more cilia. From the bronchioles they further divide into alveolar ducts which in turn become air sacs or alveoli. This is what is known as lung tissue.

*Exchange of gases between the lung and capillary*

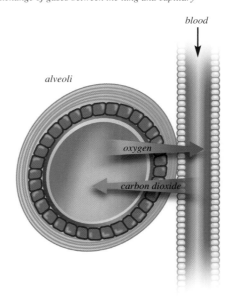

blood

alveoli

oxygen

carbon dioxide

capillary

The alveoli contain fine capillaries that are branches of the pulmonary artery and it is through these that the gaseous exchange of oxygen and carbon dioxide occurs. These alveoli have a huge surface area that is estimated at several hundred square metres.

Oxygen diffuses from the air into the alveoli and combines with haemoglobin. The remaining carbon dioxide is expelled as the horse exhales.

The ribs and the diaphragm return to their original position, the size of the chest is reduced and pressure on the lungs increases, forcing the air out.

The resting breath rate of an adult horse is 10 – 15 breaths per minute (bpm) but this quickly goes up to 25 bpm when the horse is asked to move. At maximum exercise the respiration rate can reach 130 bpm. After exercise the respiration rate will gradually return to normal. Fitness is defined by how quickly the respiration and heart rates return to normal after exertion.

### Defence of the respiratory system

When grazing, the horse's head is below the base of the neck. In this position the trachea slopes downwards. Any mucus drains down from the trachea into the throat from which it can be swallowed. If the mucus is excessive, as after hard exercise, it may run down the nasal passages and exit through the nostrils.

With this in mind it follows that feeding from the floor is the best thing for the horse not only to protect their respiratory system but also to help with their musculature.

## The large intestine

Food passes from the small intestine into the large intestine or caecum and large colon via the ileocaecal valve (see right). Here micro-bacteria break it down into its basic constituents. A large proportion of the water taken in by the horse from its food is re-absorbed in the large intestine. The large colon folds over on itself and narrows at one point which is the most likely part of the large intestine to become blocked. The large intestine feeds into the small colon, rectum and anus.

## The hind limbs

Whereas the fore feet are prone to lameness, disfunction in the back or hind legs creates more back or hock problems. The hind foot is narrower and more upright than the fore enabling it to dig into the ground when propulsion is required. The sole of the hind foot is also a little more concave than that of the fore foot.

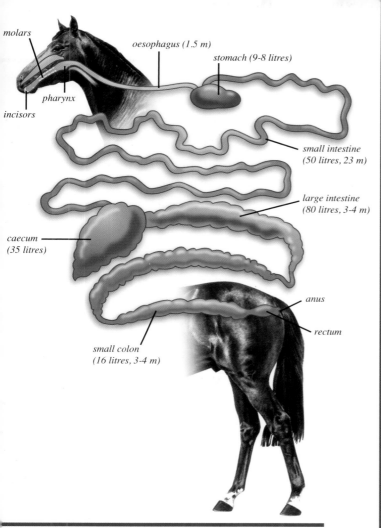

molars
oesophagus (1.5 m)
stomach (9-8 litres)
pharynx
incisors
small intestine
(50 litres, 23 m)
large intestine
(80 litres, 3-4 m)
caecum
(35 litres)
anus
rectum
small colon
(16 litres, 3-4 m)

The horse's digestive system.

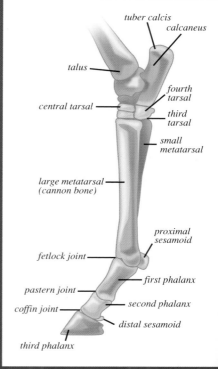

Side view of the bones of the horse's hind limb.

tuber calcis
calcaneus
talus
fourth tarsal
central tarsal
third tarsal
small metatarsal
large metatarsal
(cannon bone)
proximal sesamoid
fetlock joint
first phalanx
pastern joint
coffin joint
second phalanx
distal sesamoid
third phalanx

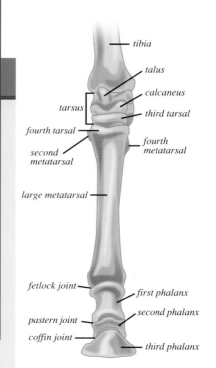

Front view of the bones of the horse's hind limb.

tibia
talus
calcaneus
tarsus
third tarsal
fourth tarsal
fourth tarsal
second metatarsal
fourth metatarsal
large metatarsal
fetlock joint
first phalanx
pastern joint
second phalanx
coffin joint
third phalanx

## The bones and joints of the hind limbs

### Exclusive to the hind limbs:

- Femur
- Stifle – equivalent to the human knee
- Tibia and fibula fuse at their lower end ending at the hock

### Common to fore and hind limbs:

- three carpals – cannon and two splint bones. These are known as metacarpals on the front legs and metatarsals on the hind legs
- first phalanx – long pastern
- second phalanx – short pastern
- third phalanx – pedal bone/coffin bone

## Femur

This is the strongest bone in the body and the largest of the long bones in the horse. The joint between the pelvis and the femur is known as the hip joint.

This is best seen when the leg is flexed and produces a wide range of movement. The hip joint is a ball and socket joint (this enables flexion, extension, adduction and abduction motions).

### The hip joint:

- provides a site for muscle attachment
- allows the efficient transfer of force to the spine
- provides attachments for muscles of the hindquarters

## Stifle

The stifle is made up of three joints formed by the union between the femur and tibia and the femur and patella. It helps to distribute the effects of concussion through all the large muscle masses to which it is attached. It can suffer damage similar to that of the human knee such as cartilage damage, dislocation and inflammation.

### These problems can be due to:

- Hereditary unsoundness
- Strain or overwork
- Injury from outside forces

This is the largest joint and also a potentially weak point during flexion and extension.

## Hock

The hock is made up of several bones. Of these, six short flat bones are arranged in approximately two rows and together they absorb concussion. There is little movement between them.

The calcaneus is the largest bone in the hock with a large upstanding process – the os calcis. The hock joint is one of the hardest working structures in the body and works in synchronisation with the stifle – they both flex at the same time and extend at the same time which therefore questions the results of a flexion test.

### The following factors will affect soundness in the stifle and hock

1. The natural angle of both joints ie the conformation of the horse
2. The condition of the synovial membranes
3. Maturity and nutrition
4. The age at which the animal first performs strenuous work
5. Whether the horse is shod and at what age this first occurred

## Patella

The patella is the horse's kneecap. It differs from ours by being able to lock into place, as part of the stay apparatus. This enables the horse to sleep whilst standing, using minimal muscular effort.

## Muscles of the hindquarters (appertaining to the Metal Element)

Individual muscles are the practitioner's primary source of location of points on the meridians and it is important to know where they originate from and go to, as well as their function

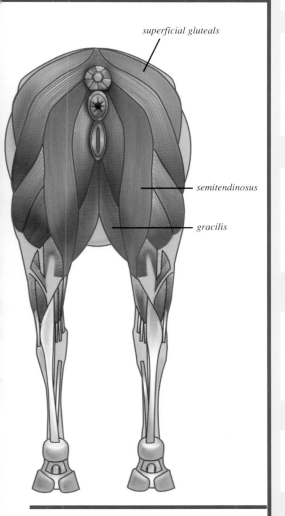

*A rear view of the muscles of the hindquarters of importance in a Shiatsu treatment.*

### Semimembranosus

| Origin | vertebral head: |
|---|---|
| | first caudal vertebra; |
| | sacrosciatic ligament |
| | pelvic head: |
| | ventro-medial aspect of ischial tuber |
| Insertion | medial condyles of femur and tibia |
| Functions | limb supporting weight: |
| | extends hip and stifle joints |
| | limb not supporting weight: |
| | retracts, adducts and rotates limb inward. |

### Semitendinosus

| Origin | vertebral head: |
|---|---|
| | last sacral and first two caudal vertebrae: |
| | tail fascia and sacrosciatic ligament; |
| | pelvic head: |
| | ventral aspect of ischial tuber |
| Insertion | cranial border of tibia; crural fascia; via tarsal tendon on calcaneus |
| Functions | limb supporting weight: |
| | extends hip, stifle and hock joints |
| | limb not supporting weight: |
| | flexes stifle, retracts and adducts limb |

### Gatsrocnemius

| Origin | With medial and lateral heads from corresponding supracondylar tuberosities of femur |
|---|---|
| Insertion | as part of common calcanean tendon on calcanean tuber |
| Functions | extends hock, flexes stifle |

### Long digital extensor

| | |
|---|---|
| Origin | lateral condyle of femur |
| Insertion | extensor process of distal (3) phalynx (secondarily on proximal and middle phalanges) |
| Functions | extends digit and flexes hock |

### Lateral digital extensor

| | |
|---|---|
| Origin | lateral collateral ligament of stifle and nearby tibia and fibula |
| Insertion | joins long extensor tendon |
| Functions | extends digit, flexes hock |

### Deep digital flexor

| | |
|---|---|
| Origin | lateral tibial condyle |
| Insertion | plantar on distal phalynx |
| Functions | extends hock and flexes digit |

### Lateral digital flexor

| | |
|---|---|
| Origin | caudal surface of tibia with tibialis caudalis |
| Insertion | plantar on distal phalanx |
| Functions | extends hock and flexes digit |

### Gracilis

| | |
|---|---|
| Origin | pelvic symphysis via symphysial tendon |
| Insertion | crural fascia, medial patellar ligament and cranial border of tibia |
| Functions | adducts limb, extends stifle |

*Key*
*C = cervical vetebrae*
*T = thoracic vertebrae*
*L = lumbar vertebrae*
*S = sacral vertebrae*

*Adapted from Anatomy of the Horse by*
*Klaus Dieter Budras, W G Sack and Sabine Rock.*

# The Water Element

## Governing the Kidney and Bladder Meridians

In Chi's creative cycle, Water is the final element, symbolised by winter, and a time of replenishment. Whilst this is the end of things it is also the beginning, a time when everything is poised ready to commence the cyclical process once again.

Reflecting the cold, still season of winter, water is the definitive Yin element. Yet there is a seed of optimism here, a feeling of contained potential. This is also a flexible element – visualise the way in which Water is able to fill any container into which it is poured. Supported in the creative cycle by Metal that brings transformation and substance to Water, this element precedes Wood. Its relationship with Wood is one of nourishment and growth. If you think of the strength and power of a flood you will understand that the Water Element has an inner strength which enables it to act as the control for the Fire Element, the definitive Yang element. Water, in its turn is controlled by Earth that blocks its way.

The characteristics of this element and the signs of balance and imbalance can be used as indications of direction towards the appropriate meridians for treatment and also as tools to help you understand your horse on a daily basis.

## Characteristics of the water element

| | |
|---|---|
| Season: | Winter |
| Time of day: | Night |
| Energy quality: | Floating |
| Colour: | Black/blue |
| Smell: | Putrid |
| Taste: | Salty |
| Sense: | Hearing |
| High Tide Time: | 3pm – 7pm<br>(Bladder 3pm - 5pm/Kidney 5pm - 7pm) |
| Emotion: | Fear |
| Voice Tone: | Groaning |
| Tissue: | Bones |
| Concepts: | Flow, power, will, life force |

## Signs of balance/imbalance

### Signs of balance
- a strong sense of direction
- courageous
- well grounded
- fluid and able to go with the flow

### Signs of imbalance
- timid, fearful, phobic
- defensive and insecure
- stressed
- a negative outlook

*Be patient and persevere with the Water horse and he will reward you with loyalty.*

# Recognising the Water horse

## Characteristics
- This horse requires a keeper who will give him confidence as, of all the elements, the Water horse is likely to be the most timid.
- Be sure to question any misbehaviour exhibited by this horse as the cause is most likely to be fear and punishment would only reinforce his fearful beliefs.

- This horse will take a long time to build up a trusting partnership with his owner or handler as he is naturally suspicious.
- In the field he is likely to keep himself to himself.
- All this perseverance and patience is worth the effort as the Water horse is a one-to-one horse and very loyal.

### Health

- This horse is prone towards arthritic problems.
- Keep an eye on his legs, pelvis and neck as the Water horse will be inclined towards 'bony' abnormalities.

### Training

- Be patient with the Water horse as he is likely to bottle up his anxieties and be inward looking, but will eventually reward you with flashes of great talent.
- Take your time training the Water horse and persevere. Once he understands and is sure of what is being asked of him he is a reliable horse.
- Be sure your aids and commands are absolutely clear and consistent with this horse as any confusion will cause him to introvert.

### Horse/rider relationship

The Water rider who has overcome her own fears will instinctively understand this horse's timidity and fear. She will be able to get the best out of this horse.

Both the Fire and Metal riders will use intuition to assess this horse's feelings and respond appropriately.

He is not suitable for the nervous Earth rider, who would not be able to give him the support and understanding he needs nor would the forceful Wood rider, focusing on her own skills and ambitions, find him to her taste.

## The Water Meridians

### The Bladder Meridian

The Bladder Meridian starts at the inside corner of the eye (medial canthus). It travels over the skull (cranium) parallel to the topline, in between the ears and closer to the side you are working, to the wing of the atlas and down the side of the neck to a point just above the shoulder blade (scapula). Here it splits into two branches. The inner branch is 1.5 cun away from the topline. Along its length, it contains the organ association points or Yu points. The outer branch is 3 cun towards the belly from the topline. The meridian continues down the back, to the outside of the hock, and then passes down the back of the outside of the pastern where it ends at a point just above the coronet band, two thirds of the distance from the centre front to the centre back of the hoof.

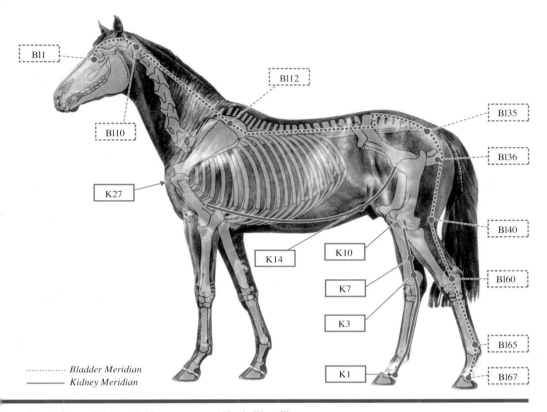

.............. *Bladder Meridian*
———— *Kidney Meridian*

*The Bladder and Kidney Meridians are governed by the Water Element.*

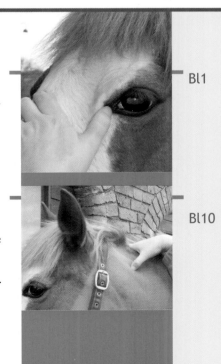

## Bladder 1 (Bl1)

This is a calming point at the inside corner of the eye in an indentation.

Indications: conjunctivitis, keratitis.

## Bladder 10 (Bl10)

Also known as Fu Tu (wing of the atlas)

This is at the top of the neck, in a depression, behind the wings of the atlas.

Indications: cervical rigidity and pain, wobbler syndrome.

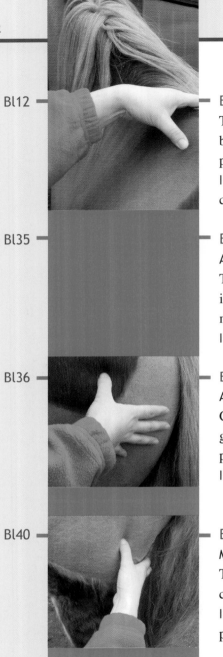

**Bl12**

**Bl35**

**Bl36**

**Bl40**

**Bl60**

### Bladder 12 (Bl12)

This is located 1 cun away from the spinous processes between the 4th and 5th thoracic vertebrae at the highest point of the withers.

Indications: cervical pain and pain in the back, cold, cough, fever.

### Bladder 35 (Bl35)

**Also known as Hui Yang (meeting of Yang)**

This is found at the base of the tail, slightly lower to its insertion between the biceps femoris and semitendinosus muscle.

Indications: pain in the hindquarters, arthritis of the hip.

### Bladder 36 (Bl36)

**Also know as Xie Chi (evil Chi)**

Continuing downward and remaining in the muscular groove between the biceps femoris and semitendinosus this point is 1 cun upwards from the point of buttock.

Indications: rotated pelvis, pain in hind limb

### Bladder 40 (Bl40)

**Master point for the lumbar and sacral section of the back**

This is on the surface of the hind leg in between the joint created by the femur and the tibia.

Indications: arthritis of the stifle and hip, lumbar back pain, cystitis, ovarian problems, urinary incontinence.

### Bladder 60 (Bl60)

**Also known as Kun Lun (lateral hock)**

This is a point that unites the neck, shoulder and back and is found between the end of the tibia and the hock bone in a hollow created by soft tissue.

Indications: back pain, hock problems.

## Bladder 65 (Bl65)

This is found slightly to the side (tail edge) of the lower end of the outside splint bone.

Indications: laminitis, tendonitis of the fetlock.

Bl65

## Bladder 67 (Bl67)

Ting point

This is found on the hind limb, just above the coronet band, two thirds of the distance between centre front and centre back of the hoof.

Indications: all hoof problems, bladder control, back and hock problems.

Bl67

## Yu points

The Yu points of the Bladder Meridian start at the 7th intercostal space, 1.5 cun down from the topline on the back edge of the scapula and continue down to the sacral foramina. There are 14 points along the length of the back.

# The Kidney Meridian

The Kidney Meridian begins between the bulbs of the heel of the hind leg and runs almost along the back of the inside of the leg. It passes internally and emerges on the abdomen forward of the pubis of the pelvic bone.

It runs towards the head along the abdomen 0.5 cun parallel to the midline, along the inside of the forelimb and ends between the sternum and the first rib.

## Kidney 1 (K1)

Also known as Hou Jiu (the central bulb)

Ting point

This is in a depression between the bulbs of the heel of the hind limb and is a grounding point for the horse.

Indications: shock, high fever, pain in heel.

K1

K3

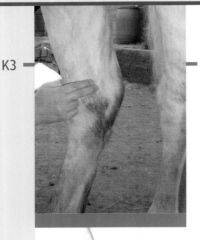

## Kidney 3 (K3)

This is found on the inside of the leg between the end of the tibia and the hock bone in the depression between the medial malleolus and the tendocalcaneus at the level of the tip of the medial malleolus. This point can be worked at the same time at Bl60.

Indications: local swelling of the hock, kidney disfunction, oestrous cycle irregularity.

K7

## Kidney 7 (K7)

Situated 2 cun above K3 on the calcaneous tendon.
Indications: hock pain, anxiety, oestral problems.

K10

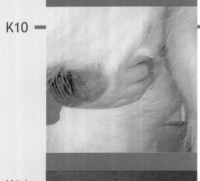

## Kidney 10 (K10)

At the joint where the femur and tibia meet on the inside of the leg between the semimembranosus and semitendinosus muscles at the level of Bl40.
Indications: lethargy, tonification point.

K14

## Kidney 14 (K14)

This is 0.5 cun to the side of the midline and 2 cun rearwards of the umbilicus.
Indications: urinary incontinence, abdominal pain.

## Kidney 27 (K27)

Primary Yu point
This is found between the sternum and the first rib.
Indications: cough, breathing problems, chest pain.

Bladder 1.

2.

## Stretches for the Water Element

### Bladder

1. Stand at a 45 degree angle to the back legs of the horse, facing the tail, and pick the back leg up, resting your outside elbow on your outside knee.
2. Moving from your ankles, gently circle the leg left, right and in a figure of eight.
3. Step backwards towards the head and stretch the leg well under the belly and adduct. Drop your bottom to the floor and encourage the leg to stretch by stroking from thigh to hoof. Do not pull the leg, just help the horse move his leg into your hand, stroking will encourage him.
4. Tuck the horse's head in and lower neck.

3.

4.

Kidney 1.

2.

## Kidney

1. Stand at a 45 degree angle to the back legs of the horse, facing the tail, and pick the hind leg up, resting your outside elbow on your outside knee. Moving from your ankles, gently circle the leg left, right and in a figure of eight.

2. Step backwards. Stretch the leg forward and slightly abduct.
3. Change your holding hand and stroke down the Kidney Meridian.
4. Stretch the belly with your hands moving outwards or palming with little stretches.

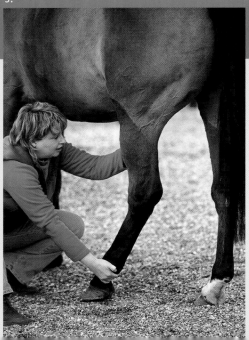
3.

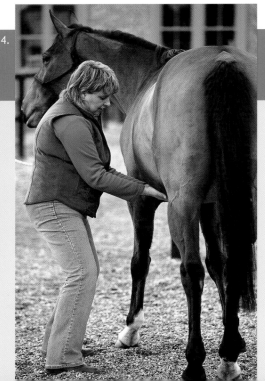
4.

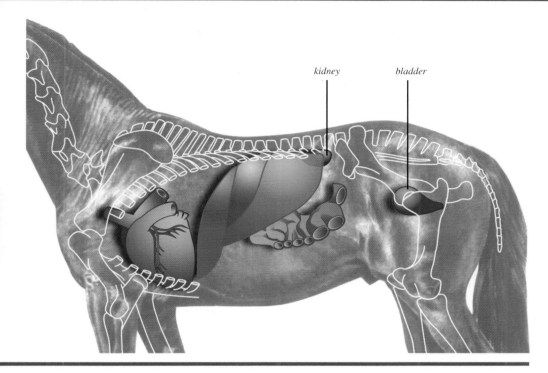

*Position of the bladder and the kidneys.*

## The urinary system

Both the kidneys and the bladder are part of the urinary system that is primarily involved in the extraction and removal of waste products from the blood. It is also involved with the balance of water content in the horse, telling him when to drink and when his thirst is satiated.

The urinary system consists of:
- 2 kidneys
- 2 ureters
- 1 bladder
- 1 urethra

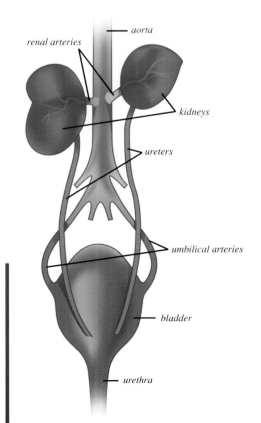

*The organs which make up the horse's urinary system.*

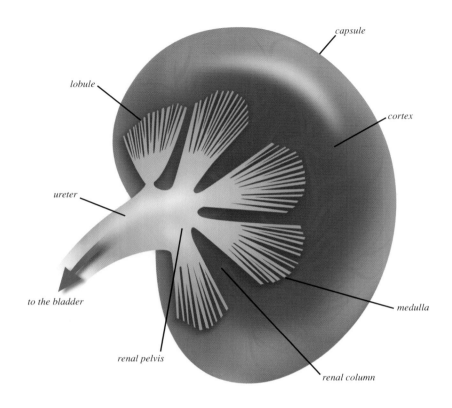

*capsule*

*lobule*

*cortex*

*ureter*

*to the bladder*

*medulla*

*renal pelvis*

*renal column*

*Around the renal pelvis is the medulla, which looks slightly furrowed due to the radially arranged collecting vessels or tubules. The cortex, which is a major secreting area, is the next layer and has a velvety and granular texture that is caused by filtering capsules called glomeruli.*

## The kidney

### Functions of the kidney

- To regulate homeostasis:
  helping to keep the correct fluid, salt and ph balance by re-absorption.
- To sieve plasma from the blood
- To clean toxins from the blood
- To secrete certain hormones including those responsible for controlling red blood cell production and calcium levels in the body.

The kidneys are situated high up against the roof of the abdomen, midway between the withers and croup, under the spine. The left kidney, which is bean shaped, lies farther back towards the last rib and the right kidney, which is heart shaped, lies under the last three ribs. They lie outside the abdominal cavity but are connected to the upper wall of the abdomen by a layer of peritoneum, which prevents them moving and they can often be surrounded by large fatty deposits that act as buffers, protecting them from injury. Despite common misconception it is therefore unusual for them to become bruised. In an adult Thoroughbred horse each kidney weighs around 700g (23oz) and measures 15 – 18cm in length. The indented portion of the kidneys is known as the hilus, this is where the blood vessels and nerves enter and the ureter and lymphatic vessels leave.

Between 1 – 2000 litres of fluid are processed daily through the kidneys which act like a filtration plant, getting rid of any impurities in the form of 5-15 litres of urine being excreted daily. The body needs much of the remainder of these fluids as they are 'cleaned' by the kidneys before being reabsorbed.

## The bladder

The bladder is a sack made of fibrous tissue that allows it to expand and contract according to the quantity of urine contained therein. When empty, it lies on the floor of the pelvis, held in place by an incomplete covering of peritoneal membrane. The remainder is covered with pelvic fascia. It has a strong muscular outer layer, the fibres of which form a circle at the 'neck' to create a sphincter muscle. As it fills with urine, the walls stretch and become thinner and the bladder moves towards the abdominal cavity. When the bladder is full, signals are sent to the central nervous system and in re-sponse the sphincter muscle relaxes, the bladder contracts and the urine is expelled.

## The other organs of the urinary system are:

### The ureter
This is a tube that extends backwards and downward from the renal pelvis of the kidney to the neck of the bladder. The ureter has a fibrous outer layer, muscular middle layer and is lined by a mucous membrane. Each kidney has its own ureter leading to the bladder. Peristalsis (muscular contractions) moves urine along the ureter.

### The urethra
This tube runs from the neck of the bladder to the outside. In the female it is fairly short opening in the floor of the vestibule within the vagina. In the male it is much longer, extending to the tip of the penis.

Disorders of the urinary system include:
**Cystitis**
   inflammation of the bladder
**Nephritis**
   inflammation of the kidneys
**Urinary calculi**
   stones
**Leptospirosis**
   infection of the kidneys, reproductive tract
   and eye tissue
**Ruptured bladder in foals**

## The composition of urine

Urine is alkaline because of the mineral content of grasses. Hay and hard feed may change pH to slightly acidic as a result of protein breakdown. A healthy horse will excrete an average of just over 5 litres every 24 hours, but this depends on factors such as fluid intake and exercise.

### The average composition of urine is:
96%  water

  2%  urea (the by product of protein metabolism)

  2%  salts

There may also be some bile and hormones.

In the event of an infection, urine will also contain toxins eliminated from the system by the kidneys. Although it contains large quantities of calcium carbonate crystals, the urine of a healthy horse is more or less clear and free from offensive odour.

### Discolouration of the urine may indicate disorders:
- It is dark red to near black coloured with muscle pigment myoglobin when azoturia has occurred
- If blood coloured, then urinary calculi (stones) may be present
- An odour may indicate infection.

*The two layers of the adrenal glands.*

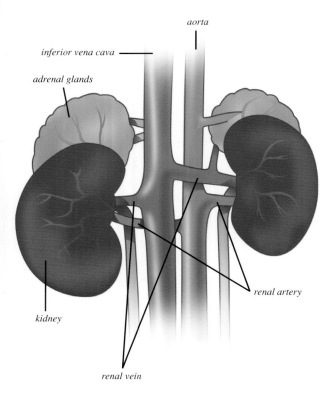

aorta

inferior vena cava

adrenal glands

renal artery

kidney

renal vein

## The adrenal glands

These two glands lie close to the kidneys, and each has two layers. The outer layer produces steroid hormones. The inner layer produces adrenalin and noradrenalin. The sympathetic nervous system directly controls the secretion of these hormones which:
- accelerates the heart
- constricts arteries
- dilates bronchioles
- dilates iris
- slows gut movements
- contracts the bladder and anal sphincter
- increases sweat secretion

# The forelimbs and shoulder

Lameness is more common in a forelimb than a hind due to the weight-bearing function of forelegs and impact such as jumping. The front limbs are attached to the axial skeleton not by bone but by soft tissue. This has a shock absorbing effect.

The bones of forelimbs
Exclusive to the fore legs:

- Scapula or shoulder blade
- Humerus
- Radius and ulna
- Carpus or knee

Common bones
to both fore and hind legs:

- three carpals – cannon and two splint bones. These are known as metacarpals on the front legs and metatarsals on the hind legs
- first phalanx – long pastern
- second phalanx – short pastern
- third phalanx – pedal bone or coffin bone

## Scapula
or shoulder blade

This is a large, triangular flat bone that lies over the outside of the first six or seven ribs from which it is separated by underlying muscles. It is also known as the wing bone.

## Humerus

This is a bone in the foreleg that lies between the end of the shoulder blade (scapula) and the elbow joint. Being relatively short and thick it is one of the strongest bones in the body. From its attachment to the shoulder blade it slopes backwards to meet the radius and form the elbow joint. It is this angle that provides in shock absorbency. It is also a site for many muscle attachments.

## Radius and ulna

These are fused together in the horse. The radius of the horse is larger than the ulna (the reverse is true in a human).

## Carpus or knee

Connecting the foreleg to the lower leg, the carpus consists of seven bones most of which are flat and fitted with wide, smooth, articular surfaces, joined together by ligaments. Their main job is shock absorption.

## Metacarpal bones

These consist of two splint and one cannon bone which together make up the metacarpus. Only one of them is fully functional (the cannon bone). The splints, or small metacarpals, on either side of the cannon bone merely help to support the knee bones and represent the remains of two digits once possessed by horses of the past. It is by measuring around these three bones that we assess a horse's ability to bear weight.

The phalanges

There are three of these bones of the foot:
1. The first phalanx or long pastern bone
2. The second phalanx or short pastern bone
   This lies partly inside the hoof and partly
   above it at the coronet.
3. The third phalanx or pedal bone
   This lies entirely within the hoof.

Sesamoid bones

These are three small bones in the horse's
lower leg. The two proximal sesamoids are
small pyramid shaped bones at the back
of the fetlock joint and are integral to the
suspensory system of the horse. The third
or distal sesamoid is better known as the
navicular bone. This is located behind the
pedal bone.

Joint and their actions

Hinge joint:
   this moves only in one plane and has flexion and extension without lateral or rota-
   tory movement eg pastern.

Ball and socket joint:
   this joint is capable of all round movement,
   only restricted by its neighbouring bones,
   ligaments and muscles eg hip.

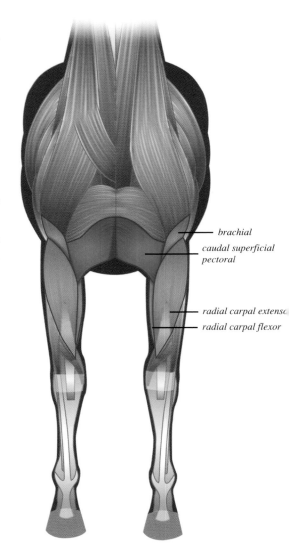

brachial

caudal superficial
pectoral

radial carpal extenso

radial carpal flexor

*The muscles of the shoulder*
*and the forelimb of importance in Shiatsu.*

# Superficial muscles of the shoulder and forelimb

Individual muscles are the practitioner's primary source of location of points on the meridians and it is important to know where they originate from and go to, as well as their function.

## Trapezius-cervical

| | |
|---|---|
| Origin | nuchal and supraspinous ligaments from C2-T10 |
| Insertion | scapular spine |
| Functions | elevates shoulder, draws scapula up and forwards (cranio dorsally) and up and backwards (caudo dorsally) |

## Deltoid

| | |
|---|---|
| Origin | clavicular inscription |
| Insertion | crest of humerus |
| Function | advances limb |

## Triceps

| | |
|---|---|
| Origin | backward edge (caudal border) of scapula, deltoid tuberosity, medial surface of humerus |
| Insertion | olecranon tuber |
| Function | extends elbow joint and flexes shoulder joint |

## Extensor carpi radialis

| | |
|---|---|
| Origin | lateral supracondylar crest and radial fossa |
| Insertion | proximodorsal on metacarpal 3 |
| Functions | extends knee (carpus) |

## Oblique carpal extensor

| | |
|---|---|
| Origin | top outside (cranilateral) middle of radius |
| Insertion | proximal on metacarpal 2 |
| Function | extends knee (carpus) |

## Extensor carpi ulnaris

| | |
|---|---|
| Origin | lateral epicondyle of humerus |
| Insertion | short tendon: accessory carpal bone long tendon: proximal on metacarpal 4 |
| Function | flexes knee (carpus) |

## Common digital extensor

| | |
|---|---|
| Origin | lateral epicondyle of humerus |
| Insertion | proximodorsal on proximal phalanx |
| Function | carpal and digital extensor |

## Lateral digital extensor

| | |
|---|---|
| Origin | top end of radius and ulna |
| Insertion | proximodorsal on proximal phalanx |
| Function | extensor of fetlock joint (not digit) |

Key
C = cervical vetebrae    L = lumbar vertebrae
T = thoracic vertebrae   S = sacral vertebrae

Taken from Anatomy of the Horse by
Klaus Dieter Budras, W G Sack and Sabine Rock.

# Part 4

# Appendices

## Introduction

I have great pleasure in using, in this book, work that my two-year students have submitted as part of their course work. All students on the course have to work at home not only with theory but on practical experience as well. In this section are two case studies from Ticky Fletcher and a well researched chart of some basic treatment points from Vicky Raymond, both now practitioners in their own right. Well done to them.

# Appendix 1 Treating the correct points

Here's an introduction to meridian points that will help with the more common problems you may encounter.

## A

| Analgesia point | TH5 | | | |
|---|---|---|---|---|
| Anorexia | St36 | | | |
| Arthritis of the carpal joint | Ht7 | | | |
| Arthritis of the fetlock | Bl65 | | | |
| Arthritis of the foreleg | GB21 | SI3 | Sp3 | |
| Arthritis of the hindquarters | Bl35 | Bl36 | | |
| Arthritis of the hip/stifle | Bl35 | St34 | St45 | |
| Arthritis - metacarpal | Lu9 | | | |
| Arthritis of the neck | Bl60 | | | |
| Arthritis of the shoulder | SI11 | SI14 | LI15 | |
| Arthritis of the tarsal joint | St36 | | | |
| Arthritis of the thoracic limb | SI11 | SI14 | LI15 | |
| Asthma | K27 | Lu9 | | |

## B

| Back and hock problems | Bl67 | St41 | | |
|---|---|---|---|---|
| Back disorders/pain | Bl60 | Sp21 | Lu1 | Lu9 |
| Back, strengthens caudal and extremities | GB34 | | | |
| Bladder control | Bl67 | | | |
| Bone healing | Bl11 | | | |

# C

| | | | | | | | |
|---|---|---|---|---|---|---|---|
| Calms the mind | HP6 | Bl14 | Bl15 | | | | |
| Cervical rigidity and pain | Bl10 | | | | | | |
| Chest pain | Li14 | GB21 | HP1 | K27 | Ht1 | Lu1 | Lu9 |
| Cold | GB20 | LI20 | | | | | |
| Colic | TH1 | St45 | | | | | |
| Conjunctivitis | GB1 | Bl1 | St1 | | | | |
| Convulsions | Li3 | TH1 | | | | | |
| Corneal ulcers | St1 | | | | | | |
| Cough | SI11 | LI20 | Lu1 | Lu5 | Lu9 | | |

# D

| | | |
|---|---|---|
| Diarrhoea | SP9 | ST25 |
| Distal extremities - pain | GB40 | |

# E

| | | |
|---|---|---|
| Earthing/calming point | K1 | SI3 |
| Emphysema | Sp21 | |
| Eye pain | LI11 | |
| Eye problems | Li3 | |

# F

| | | | | | | | |
|---|---|---|---|---|---|---|---|
| Facial paralysis and tension | SI19 | St1 | St4 | St6 | Lu7 | | |
| Facial swelling | St4 | St6 | | | | | |
| Fear | HP3 | | | | | | |
| Fetlock tendinitis | Sp3 | Lu9 | | | | | |
| Fever | GB20 | TH1 | HP3 | SI1 | LI1 | LI4 | LI11 | LI20 |

| | | | | | |
|---|---|---|---|---|---|
| Foot and hoof problems | HP1 | HP9 | St45 | LI1 | Lu11 |

## G

| | | | | | |
|---|---|---|---|---|---|
| Gastrointestinal and urinary disorders | Sp6 | St25 | St36 | | |

## H

| | | | | | |
|---|---|---|---|---|---|
| Heel pain | K1 | | | | |
| Heel inflamation | Ht9 | Lu11 | | | |
| Heart - important point | HP6 | | | | |
| Heat stroke | GB1 | | | | |
| Hepatitis | Li14 | | | | |
| Hock pain | Li3 | GB40 | | | |
| Hock swelling and problems | K3 | Bl60 | | | |
| Hoof problems - hind | Bl67 | | | | |
| Hypersalivation | St4 | | | | |

## I

| | | | | | |
|---|---|---|---|---|---|
| Immunostimulation | St36 | LI4 | LI11 | Lu11 | |
| Indigestion | LI10 | | | | |

## K

| | | | | | |
|---|---|---|---|---|---|
| Keratitis | BL1 | St1 | | | |
| Kidney and urogenital problems | GB25 | | | | |
| Kidney dysfunction | K3 | | | | |

## L

| Laminitis | Li1 | GB40 | TH1 | Bl65 | SI1 | SI3 |
| --- | --- | --- | --- | --- | --- | --- |
| | Ht9 | Sp1 | St45 | LI1 | Lu9 | Sp21 |
| Lethargy | K10 | St36 | LI20 | | | |
| Lingual paralysis | St4 | | | | | |
| Liver disorders | Sp21 | | | | | |
| Loin and hip pain | St34 | | | | | |
| Lumbar pain | GB25 | | | | | |
| Lung function - promotion | St6 | | | | | |
| Lung congestion | LI20 | | | | | |

## M

| Master point for head and neck | LI4 | Lu7 | | | | |
| --- | --- | --- | --- | --- | --- | --- |
| Master point for the caudal back | Bl40 | | | | | |
| Master point of the cranial tibia muscle | St36 | | | | | |
| Master point for obstetric problems | Sp6 | | | | | |
| Mastication problems | St4 | St6 | | | | |
| Maxillary and mandibular disorders | St4 | St6 | | | | |
| Milk production - poor | SI1 | | | | | |
| Muscle and abdomenal soreness | Li13 | Li14 | GB24 | St41 | | |
| Myositis of the thigh and rump muscles | GB29 | GB30 | | | | |

## N

| Neck pain | GB20 | GB21 | TH5 | LI4 | Lu7 | Bl10 |
| --- | --- | --- | --- | --- | --- | --- |
| Nosebleeds | Lu11 | | | | | |

## O

| Oedema of the cranial thorax | Lu1 | | | | | |
| --- | --- | --- | --- | --- | --- | --- |
| Oestrous cycle irregularity | K3 | Sp10 | K5 | | | |

# P

| | | | | | | | |
|---|---|---|---|---|---|---|---|
| Pain in the distal extremities | GB40 | | | | | | |
| Pain reduction | St36 | | | | | | |
| Pain/sprain of hip joint, pelvic infection | GB31 | | | | | | |
| Paralysis of the scapular nerve | Ht1 | | | | | | |
| Paralysis of the suprascapular nerve | LI15 | | | | | | |
| Paralysis of the tibial and fibular nerve | St36 | | | | | | |
| Paralysis of ulnar or radial nerve | SI9 | | | | | | |
| Patella - upward fixation | St34 | St36 | | | | | |
| Pelvic dislocation | Bl36 | | | | | | |
| Periostis | Lu9 | | | | | | |
| Pharyngitis | LI1 | LI11 | | | | | |
| Pneumonia | HP6 | | | | | | |
| Poisoning | Sp9 | | | | | | |

# R

| | | | | | | | |
|---|---|---|---|---|---|---|---|
| Radial paralysis | LI10 | | | | | | |
| Respiratory failure | Lu11 | | | | | | |
| Rhinitis | LI20 | | | | | | |
| Ringbone | St45 | LI1 | | | | | |

# S

| | | | | | | | |
|---|---|---|---|---|---|---|---|
| Sciatica | GB30 | | | | | | |
| Shock | K1 | | | | | | |
| Shoulder pain or paralysis | GB21 | TH15 | HP6 | LI14 | Lu1 | Lu9 | Ht1 |
| Shoulder problems | SI9 | | | | | | |
| Sidebone | Li1 | TH1 | St45 | LI1 | Lu11 | | |
| Sinusitis | LI20 | | | | | | |

## S

| | | | |
|---|---|---|---|
| Sore throat | Lu11 | | |
| Stifle/thigh pain | Li8 | Sp9 | Sp10 |
| Stomach harmony | HP6 | | |
| Sunstroke | LI20 | | |

## T

| | | | |
|---|---|---|---|
| Tendon contracture | TH5 | | |
| Tetanus | St4 | St6 | |
| Thoracic limb sprain | Ht1 | | |
| Throat problems | TH1 | HP6 | |
| Tibal and fibular pain | St36 | | |
| Tranquilisation | St4 | St6 | |

## U

| | | | | |
|---|---|---|---|---|
| Urinary incontinence | K14 | | | |
| Urticaria disorders | Sp9 | Sp10 | LI11 | LI20 |
| Uterine disease | Li3 | | | |
| Uterine prolapse | Li8 | | | |

## W

| | | | |
|---|---|---|---|
| Weakness in tendon and muscle atrophy | GB34 | | |
| Weakness or pain in hind limb | GB34 | | |
| Weekness-general | TH10 | Sp21 | |
| Wobbler syndrome | GB20 | TH10 | Bl10 |

# Appendix 2

## Case history 1

### Background information

Name:      Geoff
Height:    16.2hh
Sex:       Gelding
Breed:     Thoroughbred
Age:       13

Turnout situation:

Geoff lives in at night and is turned out for as much of the day as possible with one or two other horses. He tends to get injured if he is put out in larger groups as he likes to play!

Relevant history:

- Geoff has probably raced on the flat. His current owners bought him from a lady who had owned him for four to five years and he had done dressage, a little jumping and some fun rides. Geoff was being sold as his owner's husband was seriously ill.

- He has been with his current owner for three years. He has competed in dressage at Elementary/Medium level. He was lightly competed last year due to foot lameness, which has now been resolved.

- He is an easy horse to handle and likes people. He likes routine and can become upset by too much change such as alterations to his routine on competition days. Staying away from home can also make him tense. A routine has been established both at home and for competition days with which he seems to be happy. He now remains calm and relaxed and produces a good performance.

- This is not a horse to be hurried or for too much pressure to be put upon as he demonstrates signs of stress. His owner always makes sure she has plenty of time to do what is required without having to rush him. The owner works Geoff according to how he feels on a particular day. She feels they are a partnership and that he is more cheerful than he was when first purchased.

### Medical history

- There were several instances of colic in the first 18 months of ownership which were linked to stress situations. In the last 12 months there has been no colic due to changes in management and Shiatsu treatments.

- When first purchased he was treated by a physiotherapist regularly. He seemed to get small areas of muscle spasm behind the saddle and at the withers. As his musculature has developed in a more correct outline and he has received Shiatsu treatment, this has virtually stopped.

- He has an old tendon injury on the left fore, possibly from racing.

- He is on no medication.

## Visual observations

Appearance: Conformation is generally pleasing. He is slightly long in the back. His feet are rather flat. At purchase he was rather angular and lacking muscle in some places with some strange muscle development on his neck. He was not very fit at that time but his muscle tone was hard and tight, particularly in the lower neck and shoulders. It is believed this was due to being 'held together' by his riders. As a result the back of the horse had not been able to work correctly and was lacking in muscle along the topline. The muscle tone and structure has improved and he now has a pleasing rounded appearance. His coat is loose and shiny.

- He can be head shy and doesn't like having his mane plaited or pulled.

- The left hind leg is stiffer than the right and he occasionally drags this foot so the shoe becomes worn at the toe. His hind legs tend to get filled.

## Shiatsu treatment given

### 12 treatments have been given

| Treatment No | Method | Jitsu | Kyo |
|---|---|---|---|
| 1. | | Lu | LI |
| 2. | | Lu | LI |
| 3. | | LI | Bl, Lu |
| 4. | | LI, Lu | St,Sp, Bl |
| 5. | | | Ht, SI, Bl |
| 6. | | | Bl, K |
| 7. | | Lu | Bl |
| 8. | Zones | Lu, LI | St, Sp |
| 9. | Zones | Lu | St, Sp |
| 10. | Zones, Ting | St, Sp | GB, Li |
| 11. | Zones | TH, HP | St, Sp |
| 12. | | | Bl, Lu, LI, Ht, SI |

In seven treatments, the Metal Element (Lung and Large intestine) have been Jitsu with Earth (Stomach and Spleen) Kyo. In the last two treatments I have started to work through the Fire Meridians to overcome the excess Lung and Large Intestine. I have also worked with Liver and Gall Bladder to influence Stomach and Spleen (Ko cycle. Control cycle.)

- When working on Large Intestine he always seems to like work on points 10-15, which relate to the shoulder and forearm mobility and have a link to digestion. When working on Stomach and Spleen meridians he likes work across the rib cage, particularly St25 – this is the alarm point for the large intestines. He always likes me to work under his lower jaw, massaging, and stroking right up between the two branches.

## Oriental diagnosis
This is an Earth/Metal horse because:
### Earth Characteristics
- he likes being with people
- he loves his routine
- he is kind and generally grounded
### Metal Characteristics
- he has an even temper
- he is reliable in his level of performance
- he will always try if you ask in a fair way
- he has a strong vibrant expression particularly around food.

## Five Element theory:
He was Metal deficient at purchase (dislike of change, coat condition), which meant that Water was not being nourished and unable to hold Fire down (stress colic). Water was also unable to nourish Wood that was showing signs of stagnating (tendon injury, left hind stiffness).

## Conclusion
The treatments tonified Earth to nourish Metal and Water. This will help to ease the stagnation of Chi in Wood. With the treatments I have given this horse he has improved in his shape and musculature. Since Christmas people have commented how different he is to look at and he has more sparkle in himself. I feel he is much happier and content in himself. The treatments have helped to strengthen the Earth and Water elements so helping to support the Shen cycle. The horse is beginning to show some of his Fire characteristics.

## Case history 2

### Background information
Name: Poseidon
Height: 16.2 hh
Sex: Gelding
Breed: Irish Draught
Age: 11

### Turnout situation:
He lives out in the summer and is in at night in the winter

### Feed:
He easily gets overweight and this has to be watched constantly.

### Relevant history:
• Poseidon's previous owner was a breeder. From the age of five to nine he was used as a hunt horse for the whipper-in, and was therefore worked hard through the winter and rested through the summer. He had to stop hunting due to a spavin in his left hind and he could not jump. I suspect he has been handled in an unsympathetic manner.

• His current owner has had him for two years and he is used for hacking three or four times a week. He is not good in heavy traffic.

• He is a strong, chunky type of horse. He gets on well with other horses but can be a bit of a bully, particularly if he thinks there might be food about or he is missing out on something. He is not always easy to catch but if left for five minutes by himself he will stand at the gate calling to come in.

### Medical history
• There is a bone spavin in his left hind leg and Poseidon is consequently not totally sound in trot. This has not deteriorated in the last two years.

• The right forefoot has had an injury to the coronet band in the past. The wall does not grow correctly. The owner was told on purchase that he did not like having his feet picked up due to the amount of treatment he had received to this foot. He will now have his feet picked up without problems.

• He is on no medication.

### Visual observations
Conformation is generally good, but he is slightly long in the back. Hocks show thickening and puffiness but the other joints are clean. His right eye is prone to weeping particularly in windy conditions.

• Generally he is easy to handle but once he becomes upset, whether being ridden or at home, he does not easily forget about it. In these situations he can start to panic, particularly when being ridden.

When being handled he appears to get 'bolshy'. There have been a couple of occasions when on a ride he has come home without his owner being able to control him.

- In situations that do not worry him, such as being clipped, he remains quite calm.

- If he thinks he can benefit from behaving in a certain way, he will. He does not recognise his borders and boundaries. For example he will not leave the yard for a ride if he thinks he is going to be fed.

- When being ridden he can be lethargic but I feel this is taking advantage of the rider's ability, as when he chooses he can be strong and onwards bound.

- His owner cares for him well, but is not intuitive when something is beginning to go wrong, particularly when being ridden. She can be quite nervous of him when he is misbehaving which can turn to anger expressed by shouting. She can be quite single minded in her approach to some situations which brings them into conflict. I think the owner has a Wood/Water imbalance.

## Shiatsu treatment given

9 treaments have been given

| Treatment No | Method | Jitsu | Kyo |
|---|---|---|---|
| 1 | Zones | SI | Bl |
| 2. | Zones | LI | Bl, Lu |
| 3. | Zones | | Lu, LI, Sp, St |
| 4. | Zones | LI | Li |
| 5. | Zones | Lu | LI |
| 6. | Zones | Lu | LI |
| 7. | Zones & Yu | Lu, SI | Bl, K |
| 8. | Zones & Yu | Li, HP, SI | GB |
| 9. | Zones & Yu | Lu, HP, St | Sp, Bl |

I always find that the energy is patchy on him – there are parts of meridians he really likes and others he definitely does not. On occasion I find the connection is not so clear or strong. The treatments show that Metal is most commonly Jitsu or Kyo with Earth and Water Kyo.

- At treatment seven the horse had been badly frightened having been chased by a tractor down a lane and into a field. This had obviously frightened and unsettled both him and his owner. This is reflected in the Fire Meridians showing as Jitsu.

### Oriental diagnosis
This is an Earth/Metal horse because:
### Earth characteristics
- chunky, heavy body
- prone to putting on weight
- strong body, deep girth
- amiable
- can be patient
- likes routine

### He also has some Earth imbalance signs
- greedy about food
- chasing others off food
- pushy/stubborn
- heavy walk
- sensitive to damp - spavin

### Metal characteristics
- good coat
- can be rather distant
- likes orderliness

### Metal imbalance signs are
- lethargic
- confused

### Five Element theory
Poseidon is Metal deficient therefore Water is not being nourished and is becoming deficient. The owner's own Water imbalance is probably contributing to draining this element, which is why he shows signs of Water imbalance as nervousness/panic, feeding off the rider's own fears. As Water is weak it is unable to control Fire – for example when the horse had been badly frightened by the tractor.

### Conclusion
Tonify Water to help control Fire excess that will reduce its effect on Metal. Work Earth to support Water and feed Metal so you can move from the Ko to the Shen cycle. This would allow you to work on Wood and improve the flow of Chi. By working Liver and controlling Fire this would settle the Shen.

- The horse was given two weeks without being ridden and shoes taken off. The owner thought this might help him to forget about the tractor incident. In this time I carried out the last two treatments. When she started to ride him again he was much calmer. They had a successful ride where they were able to cope with meeting three large vehicles. The owner had felt 'brave' enough to ride positively past a tractor.

Update

I have done some treatments since and am finding it difficult to get on to the Liver Meridian. On the last treatment – he let me on to the Ting points and allowed me to perform stretches in the field without a headcollar on. He had come up to me in the field as I was walking through. I am finding he comes up to me in the field much more readily then previously. He is also turned out more than before although it continues to be a battle to control his weight.

He and his owner seem a lot more settled and happy.

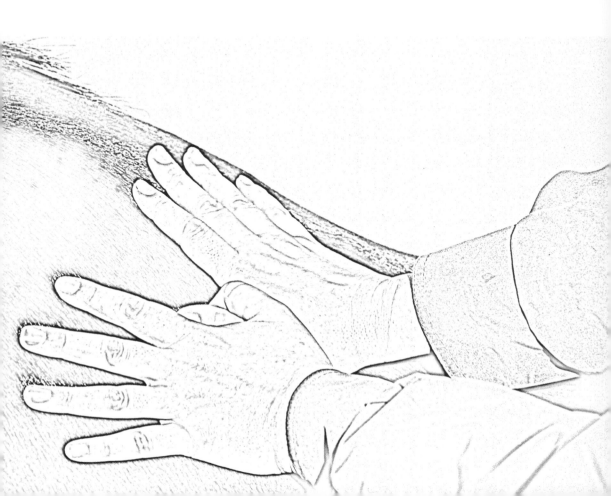

## Courses available at the College of Natural Equine Studies

If you would like to study equine Shiatsu in more depth Cathy Tindall, principal of the College for Natural Equine Studies runs a part-time two year Practitioner Course enabling students to treat horses that are owned by other people as long as veterinary approval has been given. This course provides a chance to change your career and earn a good income as well as be able to help and give something back to the horse.

This course is recognised by tESA (the Equine Shiatsu Association of which Cathy Tindall is a founder member).

Cathy Tindall and the College for Natural Equine Studies also offer a part-time two year course in Equine Behaviour, successful completion of which entitles you to treat horses that have behaviour problems. This course is accredited by the Open College Network (OCN) from whom you can gain nationally recognised credits.

Cathy also runs short clinics worldwide, all she needs is an invitation and students to teach. Please contact her via the website.

You can find out more information by looking at the website:
www.naturalequinestudies.com or www.cathytindall.com

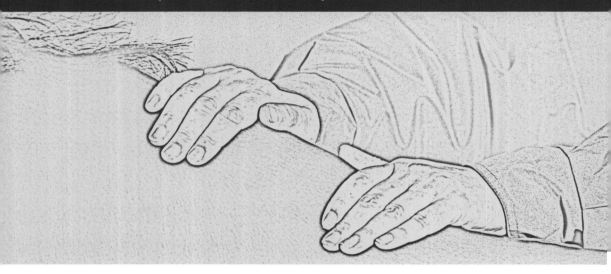

## Videos

Cathy has also produced
three videos with the horse in mind

### Equine Behaviour

Easy tips on working with various issues
demonstrated by horses

- Leading
- Lifting feet
- Calming your horse
- How to safely tie up your horse
- How to help him when he does not tie
  easily.

### Equine Shiatsu Bodywork

This is a practical guide on how to perform
the basic treatments mentioned in this
book.

### Effective Loading

Loading is one of the most common problems that Cathy is called out to help with.
This is a three-step programme guaranteed
to teach your horse to load time and time
again.

For further details please look at the website.

## Recommended reading

Veterinary Acupuncture
M. Schoen

Equine Acupressure
Nancy Zidonis

Wood Becomes Water
Gail Reichstein

Traditional Acupuncture
'The Law of the Five Elements'
Dianne M Connelly

Chinese Medicine
Tom Williams

BHS Veterinary Manual
P S Hastie

Anatomy of the Horse - 3rd edition
Klaus Dieter Budras, W G Sack
and Sabine Rock

Chinese Medicine
The Web that has no Weaver
Ted J Kaptchuk

The Horse Physiology
Julie Brega

Essential Equine Studies
Julie Brega
Book 1 Anatomy and Physiology

# Terminology

## A

**Abduction**
Taking the limb away from the midline of the body

**Acupressure**
A massage technique applying pressure to various points of the body

**Acute**
Rapid onset, severe and recognisable signs, often quick recovery after treatment.

**Adduction**
Taking the limb towards the midline of the body

**Adrenalin**
The hormone secreted from the adrenal medulla/adrenal glands and responsible for the fright/flight response

**Aerobic**
In the presence of oxygen

**Amino acids**
Chemical compounds that are the basic building blocks of all proteins

**Anaerobic**
Without the presence of oxygen

**Arterial**
Relating to an artery(ies)

**Articulation**
The point at which two or more bones join or function

**Atlas**
First cervical vertebrae supporting the skull

**Atrophy**
Wasting away

**Axial**
The part of the skeleton which consists of the vertebral column, ribs, sternum and skull

**Axis**
The second cervical vertebrae

**Azoturia**
Generally a condition of a fit horse returning to work after confined rest, that finds that his muscles become stiff and extremely sore after work. He may begin to sweat and have a staggering gait or indeed may not be able to move forward. His urine may be dark in colour.

## C

**Canthus**
Corner of the eye where the lids meet

**Cartilage**
Dense connective tissue found chiefly at joints and between bones

**Cartilaginous**
Of cartilage

**Caudo/caudal**
Towards the back end

**Chronic**
Continued or long term

**Condyloid**
A synovial joint, structured so that an oval-shaped condyle fits into an elliptical cavity of another bone

**Connective tissue**
A tissue type, with widely separated cells, that supports, protects and binds together the other tissues of the body

**Cranium**
Skull

**Cranial**
Towards the head end

**Cubital**
Relating to the elbow

**Cubital crease**
The crease created by the bending of the forearm - the joint between the humerus and the radius and the ulna

**Cun**
Half the circumference of the horse's pastern

**D**
**Distal**
Away from the trunk of the body

**Dorsal**
Of, on, near, or towards the back /topline

**E**
**Endorphins**
Pain relieving substances produced by the body

**Enzyme**
Catalysts to a specific biochemical reaction; specific protein with this function

**Epicondyle**
A prominence on a bone generally near a joint and a site for the attachment of soft tissues

**F**
**Fascia**
A fibrous membrane covering, supporting and separating muscles (and other structures)

**Fossa**
A furrow or shallow depression

**G**
**Ginglymus**
A synovial joint that only allows movement in one plane (like a door hinge) eg elbow

# H

## Haemoglobin

Made up of protein called globin and an iron-containing pigment called haemin, haemoglobin is what gives blood its red colour. Its main function is to carry oxygen from the lungs to all the tissues of the body

## Humerus

The bone between the shoulder and the elbow

# I

## Illium

The largest of the three pelvic bones

## Insertion

The point where a muscle attaches to a bone

## Intercostal

The space between the ribs, filled with nerves and muscles

## Involuntary muscle

As in the blood vessels, stomach, intestines and the heart. These are not under conscious control

## Ischium

A pelvic bone that anatomically is two separate bones

# J

## Jitsu

Full, blocked, over active

## Joint

A junction between bones

# K

## Kyo

Empty, depleted, lacking in energy

# L

## Lateral

In or towards the outside

# M

## Maxillary bone

Upper jaw bone

## Medial

In or towards the middle, inside

## Metatarsals

The bones of the hind limb from the hock to the fetlock

## Mitochondria

Rod like structures within cells, often referred to as the power plant of the cell

## Mother hand

The hand that remains still whilst the working hand moves along the meridian. The Mother hand listens and exerts a little pressure

## N

**Noradrenaline**

A precursor of adrenaline in the medull of the suprarenal glands. It is also present in the brain. Its main function is to mediate the transmission of impulses in the sympathetic nervous system

## P

**Parasympathetic nervous system**

Responsible for reverse response to sympathetic nervous system (see below): lowering the heart and respiration rate; bringing blood supply back to guts; stimulating flow of digestive juices and saliva; constriction of pupils

**Peptide**

A compound formed by the union of two or more amino acids

**Proximal**

Situated towards the trunk of the body

## S

**Scapula**

Shoulder blade

**Sympathetic nervous system**

Part of the nervous system responsible for the fright/flight response: quickened heart rate and respiration; blood diversion to muscles; evacuation of rectum; production of sweat and dilation of pupils

## T

**Thoracic**

The forelimb of the horse

**Tubercle**

A small rounded process on a bone (or other structure)

**Tuberosity**

A large, rough somewhat rounded process on a bone

## U

**Unilateral**

Affecting one side only

**Ventral**

Towards or near the stomach or lower body surface

**Voluntary muscle**

As in the skeletal muscles. These muscles are under conscious control